THE HAUNTED BOONSLICK

GHOSTS, GHOULS & MONSTERS OF MISSOURI'S HEARTLAND

MARY COLLINS BARILE

Haunted
America

Published by Haunted America
A Division of The History Press
Charleston, SC 29403
www.historypress.net

Copyright © 2011 by Mary Collins Barile

All rights reserved

First published 2011

ISBN 978.1.60949.208.3

Library of Congress Cataloging-in-Publication Data

Barile, Mary.
The haunted Boonslick : ghosts, ghouls, and monsters of Missouri's heartland / Mary
Collins Barile.
p. cm.
Includes bibliographical references (p.   ).
ISBN 978-1-60949-208-3
1. Ghosts--Missouri. I. Title.
BF1472.U6B373 2011
133.109778--dc23
2011025150

This book is for Sammy, Bella, Cooper and Rascal,
who keep away the ghosts at night.

CONTENTS

PREFACE

Ghost: The sense should be fury, anger, ugly; the root in Old Norse means to rage, in the Gothic to terrify [while] *the derivatives seem to point to a primary sense "to wound, tear, pull to pieces."*
—Oxford English Dictionary

W ho knew ghosts could be so much work? Over the past several years, I have found myself sitting in the pitch black of a jail at 2:00 a.m., hoping to coax a shy spirit into chatting. I've trekked with friends up hollers and over fields in search of an old cabin said to be the scene of a spook light. I have waited patiently for a broken music box to begin tinkling and dragged recording equipment up and down dark alleys to try and catch the sounds of the past. I have slipped on ripe persimmons while trying to decipher gravestones in the Boone burying ground and met people who had met ghosts. It turns out that finding ghosts *is* difficult, but finding ghost stories is not as hard as you might think—just walk into a gathered group of Missourians in the Boonslick region, mention ghosts and after a few minutes of uncomfortable shuffling and demurring ("I don't *really* believe in spirits"), you will have more stories than you can shake a sheet at.

The Boonslick, named after a naturally occurring saline spring, is among the oldest settlement areas west of the Mississippi, and the cultural traditions here run deep. The region has vaguely defined borders, sometimes running from St. Louis across the state to Saline and Jackson Counties. Other times, the border dips down to Jefferson City or arcs downward into

The Boonslick is among the most haunted regions in Missouri.

the deep Ozarks. The region is home to the true Missourian, the "show me" individual who takes nothing—especially ghosts—at face value. Boonslickers cherish their history, and more to the point, they are proud to share it with friends.

Over the years, at meetings, concerts and community events, I heard tales about a black carriage, a headless horse and a local spook light. It was clear that there were many lesser-known, even historical, Boonslick ghosts in danger of being forgotten, of fading completely from the landscape of local history as new stories emerged to push the old tales back into the shadows. Many readers interested in ghost lore have already seen, heard, visited or pondered the sad, haunted Lemp Mansion of St. Louis, the battlefield spirits of southern Missouri or the otherworldly poetry of Patience Worth. These stories have made the jump from local lore to national attention, both in books and on screen through popular ghost-hunting television shows. I did not want to retell the same tales, and it quickly became apparent that I would not have to. We have ghosts aplenty in the Boonslick, and most of them are unknown to outsiders. And in addition to actual hauntings and visitations, Boonslickers claim a number of excellent ghost jokes, indicating that not only did the early settlers have a sense of humor but also that ghosts were a part of their daily lives on the frontier.

Welcome to Missouri's haunted heart, the *Boon*slick.

ACKNOWLEDGEMENTS

I have been so fortunate in my friends and colleagues that it is impossible to list all who have helped me locate stories, participated in interviews and trips or offered an encouraging cup of coffee during a long night of ghost writing. Some people wished to remain anonymous, but you know who you are, and you know you have my deepest appreciation.

I wish especially to thank the following people for their encouragement and support: the Baa Baa Boonville Hookers (Janet Acton, Sara Arrandale, Elinor Barrett, Susan Meadows and Karen Neely), Margaret Barile, James Cogswell, Deb Entwistle, Susan Fales, Susan Flader, Arlene Hoose, Brett Johnson, Ryan McNeil, Christine Montgomery, Phebe Nichols, Diane and Fred Oerly, Greg Olson, Nan Presser, Lucille Salerno, Matt Saltzberg, Jill Sappington, Jennie and David Schutte, Gena Scott, Mike Shaw, Betty Sieckmann and Richard Wallace.

The following groups were also gracious with their help and their time: the Friends of Historic Boonville, the Columbia Paranormal Society, Beth Meyer and Paranormal Adventures USA, the Springfield Paranormal Research Group, the State Historical Society of Missouri, Ellis Library at the University of Missouri and the Jefferson City Tourism Bureau, including Steve Picker and Marie Lacey.

Tess Montgomery provided several photographs for this book.

Special thanks to Ben Gibson and the folks at The History Press who took on this project with enthusiasm and helped me with their patience, talent and experience.

TO THE BOONSLICK

From some cause, it happens that in the western states, a tract of country gets a name, as being more desirable than any other. The hills of the land of promise were not more fertile in milk and honey than are the fashionable points of immigration. Boon's Lick was the common centre of hopes, and the common point of union for the people. Ask one of them whither he was moving, "To Boon's Lick, to be sure."
—Timothy Flint

The beginning of the Boonslick is a vague place, with some people claiming St. Charles as its home and others putting forward St. Louis and even eastward into Illinois, near the river crossings. The Boonslick Road wandered like a wraith through the center of Missouri, disappearing, reappearing, twisting and winding across town and prairie—and so did its history.

In 1804, Nathan Boone, Daniel's son, was returning home from a hunting trip when he stumbled across a salt spring not far from the Missouri River, near Arrow Rock. Salt licks—places near a spring where salt crystallized and animals gathered to lick the mineral—were important to settlers since they provided one of the few ways by which to preserve food. Not long after the discovery, Nathan, his brother and some partners began a salt-boiling operation at the spring, which became known as the Boones' Lick or Boonslick. The path leading from St. Charles, Missouri, to the lick became the Boonslick Trail, along which taverns, hotels and farms appeared, even as the Native Americans there were pushed farther west. The Boonslick region stretched north to the prairies and south to the Ozarks and held some of the richest farming land in the country. The region was also the cradle of the Santa Fe Trail, which stretched eight hundred miles from Arrow Rock to the Mexican city of faith and connected the Boonslick to the wealth and culture of the Southwest.

That ghosts were part of the Boonslick from the beginning is no surprise; anyone who traveled the route experienced the loneliness of the prairie and moonless nights under groves of trees. Clashes between immigrants and Native Americans were fierce, sudden and sometimes deadly, and no shadow was to be taken for granted. In addition, folks who settled the Boonslick brought along old Scots-Irish and German ghost stories, while the slaves added their traditions of hoodoo, conjure and root work. True to the rough pioneer "spirits," some ghost stories in the Boonslick developed from practical jokes played on nervous farmers. But no matter how much fun could be had at the expense of an unsuspecting victim, no matter how brave or pragmatic a settler, the reason folks jumped at ghost stories was because they believed in them.

Along with their old country traditions, the Boonslick settlers were beginning to appreciate the new American culture that had taken root in the generation after the Revolution. Washington Irving had written "The Legend of Sleepy Hollow" and "Rip van Winkle," introducing the ghost and spirit worlds to the American reader, and those stories, along with the popularity of gothic literature, made ghosts a strong presence in the American landscape. Ichabod Crane aside, not all ghost stories were jokes, and the ghosts and creatures of the Boonslick still provide sleepless nights for some. While Ichabod faced a headless horseman, Boonslickers faced a headless horse. Rip van Winkle met Henry Hudson's crew, but there were Mississippi River men who were just as spooky, according to Mark Twain. And still other Boonslick ghosts seem to be one of a kind, found only in this region.

Modern paranormal investigators have explored Boonslick hauntings, using sound, voice and electromagnetic detectors, video, digital recordings and personal observations, and they have compiled compelling evidence for ghostly activity. Unlike hauntings in large cities, many of the Boonslick paranormal experiences have taken place outdoors near the Missouri and Mississippi Rivers, supporting one theory that paranormal activity may increase due to the proximity of water.

Boonslick ghost stories first appeared centuries ago within the Osage, Ioway, Sauk, Fox and other Native American tribes. Ghosts and spirits visited native peoples from the other world, while in turn, shamans traveled there through trance and vision and called on the spirits for help. The earliest ghost stories in the Boonslick were recorded around the War of 1812, and many stories date from the mid-nineteenth century and later. Unlike other regions, many haunted Boonslick sites do not have anything to do with the famous or the infamous but with everyday people who are unable to move on from their place in this world. Their attachment to the Boonslick and their homes is touching, although a few spirits seem to be cursed and doomed to eternal wandering. But no matter the reason for their being here, it appears that the Boonslick is a mighty fine place for ghosts and the people who seek them.

1

NATIVE AMERICAN SPIRITS AND MONSTERS

THE PIASA

The skies above the Boonslick between the Mississippi and Missouri Rivers were filled each year with millions of birds, migrating or not, from snow geese and eagles to pigeons, parrots, pelicans and vultures. Although some of the birds were unfamiliar to white immigrants, the differences among southern, eastern and Boonslick species had more to do with color and size than anything else. That is, until explorers and others started hearing—and seeing—the great piasa bird on the Mississippi River.

The Native Americans who lived and traveled in the Boonslick may have had different religious beliefs, but many followed the idea of a manitou—an organizing, powerful spirit or creator. Big Moniteau Creek was named after the entity by white explorers, but Native American memorials to the Manitou were also found in the area by settlers. Carved into stone or painted on bluffs and rock faces were spirit portraits depicting a deity or supernatural being who protected the land and its people. A rising moon, a star and a Manitou (or perhaps a shaman figure) were depicted on the bluffs near the Missouri town of Rocheport, but among the most spectacular of the Manitou paintings was that found near Alton, Illinois. High above the Mississippi River, the painting was visible to anyone who traveled the waters, and it filled visitors with awe.

Father Jacques Marquette, missionary and explorer, wrote of his first impressions of the painting in the seventeenth century:

> *As we coasted along rocks frightful for their height and length, we saw two monsters painted on one of these rocks, which startled us at first, and on which the boldest Indian dare not gaze long. They are as large as a calf, with horns on the head like a deer, a fearful look, red eyes, bearded like a tiger, the face somewhat like a man's, the body covered with scales, and the tail so long that it twice makes the turn of the body, passing over the head and down between the legs, and ending at last in a fish's tail. Green, red, and a kind of black, are the colors employed.*

This creature would later be called the piasa (*pie-a saw*) bird, a being transformed from the rock face into a real monster that snatched unwary travelers and flew off with them to the bluffs for dinner. Debate still goes on regarding the meaning of "piasa." Some historians believe the word was taken from the French word for river bluffs, *paillisa*, while others believe it is a Native American word for a spirit creature or troll. For the Native Americans, the piasa painting may have represented not a bird at all but

The piasa bird was part monster, part spirit, and attacked from the air as recently as the 1970s. *Courtesy State Historical Society of Missouri.*

rather an underwater panther or animal spirit that ruled the streams and lakes as the thunderbird controlled the skies. The citizens of ancient Cahokia, located near modern-day Collinsville, Illinois, carved the figure of a bird man on stone tablets between AD 700 and 1400, but it is unknown whether the carving represented a god, a shaman or a real creature. Some travelers reported that the Native Americans would honor the piasa with shouts or gunfire; others mused that perhaps the painting represented a territorial marker separating one tribe's land from another's.

Adding to the stories that grew up around the piasa were those created by writers with more imagination than knowledge. Along many of the major streams and rivers could be found burial mounds or sometimes caves or terraces where the bones of the dead were left by the tribe, and this contributed to the belief by white immigrants that the piasa was a real creature that devoured its prey. This story was enlarged by writers, including John Russell, who in the 1830s published a short story about the piasa, a word he "translated" as "the bird which devours men." Russell claimed to have visited a cave near the painting, high on the cliffs above the Mississippi River. There he discovered bones he believed had been picked clean by a giant bird, despite any real evidence.

Eventually, the piasa and the thunderbird were combined into one legend of a paranormal creature that still makes appearances. Sightings—and attacks—of giant birds have been reported in the late twentieth century from Illinois to Missouri along the Mississippi River, although scientists do not believe the birds are remnants from the dinosaur age or from a spirit world. Instead, the animals have been dismissed as blue herons or turkey vultures and the witnesses labeled as undependable or unable to tell the size of a bird in flight. Still, the reports share many of the same facts, describing an immense, black-feathered bird in the skies or in a tree near the Mississippi River bluffs. In perhaps the most famous case, which occurred in 1977 in Illinois, the piasa swooped in, grabbed and lifted a child and dragged the boy across his mother's yard. The boy kicked and screamed, and finally the bird released him and flew off. Witnesses described a large black bird, but investigators dismissed the story as overinflated imagination.

One theory is that these monsters originated when native tribes stumbled across the bones of dinosaurs and ice age animals. Stories were created to explain the behemoths and were then shared as myths among tribes. But this does not explain everything. In 1819, U.S. Army troops were sent up the Missouri to establish forts along the river. This was the first time steamboats were used as transportation on the western waters, and the U.S. government

Travelers reported seeing cliff paintings of the piasa in the seventeenth century. It is possible that the piasa represented a water spirit, which still lives beneath the Mississippi River bluffs. *Courtesy State Historical Society of Missouri.*

decided to take advantage of the native peoples' supposed naiveté. The ship was painted to look like a dragon, with the steam vented through the dragon's "nose." Adding in the smoke and noise from the engines, the army officers assumed the Native Americans would run in terror. Instead, the tribes pointed and laughed at the "monster," perhaps because they had seen the real thing in the skies over Missouri and Illinois. The piasa may have once existed, but as a spirit of protection, and it remains in some form, according to legend, either in the sky or beneath the Missouri River bluffs, where it still waits until called upon by the vanished tribes.

GHOST CAMPS, REVENANTS AND OTHER SPIRITS

When white immigrants came to the Boonslick, they encountered descendants of the original inhabitants: men and women of the Osage, Sac, Fox, Shawnee, Missouri, Omaha and other Native American groups who had lived there since the Ice Age. The immigrants found bluff-top burial mounds where the Woodland Indians had settled as early as AD 400. With few exceptions, little of the native lore was recorded, and what was collected was presented from the immigrant's point of view. This resulted in many stories being lost or changed, but those stories that survived hint at a rich lore of spirits and ghosts.

Perhaps an even more frightening creature than the piasa is the snake that lives around Creve Coeur (Broken Heart) Lake, west of St. Louis. There, a giant serpent has been reported crawling from the depths of the lake and onto land, where it lurks in the underbrush. It is said to be the form of a Native American woman who loved the son of a Spanish governor. When the young man left the woman for another more acceptable to his culture, the scorned woman drowned herself in the lake. Her father, a local chieftain, cursed his daughter for leaving her people and loving the enemy. Her spirit took on the form of the serpent for eternity, and it is said that she crawls ashore to attack those unfaithful in love.

The religious beliefs of Native Americans varied widely, but those who lived in the Missouri area had strong connections with the spirit world. The Omaha and related tribes called the Milky Way their path to eternity, where life continued, but without the sadness and struggle of the living world. After death, the spirit would follow the Milky Way. Those who deserved to enjoy the afterlife were guided along the short path, while those who were to be punished were sent along a lengthy, wavy path where they suffered for a long time. The Omaha also believed that ghosts of slain warriors returned to the battlefields, and their voices were heard in the thunder as it rolled across the sky. When someone died, the camp kept bonfires burning for four evenings, giving the spirit enough light to see its way to the next world. Some Omaha told of seeing entire ghost camps of Indians join up with a living group. The ghosts would appear slowly, and a viewer had to watch for a long time before the spirits would manifest entirely. No one thought the return of ghosts odd, and when they came home, they were ignored and allowed to join the living.

The ghost that produced the most fear was one of a murdered man. These spirits would return to the camp and take revenge on the tribe. To prevent this, the body of a murdered person was buried face down, and the soles of the feet were slit, making it difficult for the ghost to walk back to the camp. Because ghosts could cause famine when they returned to visit the living, a lump of fat was placed in the hands of the dead to provide them with food. Ghosts were known to whistle, so that was not common behavior in camp, and children feared anyone who did so. Knives and running water were believed to stop ghosts from following the living, an ancient belief shared with many other cultures.

Some Missouri tribes said that if you saw a ghost, you gained the power to tell the future, including the ability to predict the death of others. Fortunately, if someone was told by a shaman that he was going to die, the victim could take steps to thwart the future. He would sit in his shelter while a healer threw water to the left and right of him. This kept the victim's spirit from finding his or her way to the door and into the night. A person who fainted was thought to have visited the spirit world and been forced to return because no other spirits would speak to her. She had, in fact, died and returned because she was not yet ready for the next world.

2

GUINEA SAM, CONJURE MAN

*The dances of the ghosts of the departed conjurers also take place at the full
moon. All I know about this is that* [a conjurer is] *able to appear in two places
at once, to take any shape, and to know what people were saying and doing when
they were miles away.*
—*Mary Alicia Owens*

Sometime in the early nineteenth century, a young boy was captured,
traded and sold in the interior of Africa and then shipped to Charleston,
South Carolina. He was only one among millions torn from their homes and
sent on the middle crossing into slavery. Whatever his given name, this man
was known as Sam for most of his life. He took the last name of Nightengale,
and when he died in 1885, he was believed to be at least ninety years old—at
least, some believed he died.

Sam's life story is a shadow, as was the case with many blacks in
nineteenth-century America. A newspaper article about Sam said he was
the slave of a Dr. Ells from Louisiana and had lived on many plantations
in the South. Sam's last name was probably adopted from an early owner;
lists of slave owners include Nightengales in Georgia and a Nightingale
plantation in South Carolina. Around Boonville, Sam was called "Guinea
Sam," hinting at his origins along the Guinea coast of Africa. Sam's arrival
in Boonville was the stuff of legends, as recorded by antiquarian Charles
van Ravenswaay:

It was back in slave times, one of them queer, blowy days in August when it was so hot the tomato bugs just curl up and die. Our old master lived in a big house on High Street and I remembers that everyone stayed close to the house trying to keep cool. Long about noon there was some steamboats what came round Cole Bend and they was loaded way down. I was sitting on my door step under my vine, fanning and trying to keep cool. I saw those boats trying to get upriver, but it was too hot to pay them no mind, so I came inside and set in my rocking chair. I must've dozed. Anyway, the next minute there was the most awful sound I ever heard. The picture of "The Last Judgment Day" fell off the wall. I thought Hell had busted its iron chains, and I ran outside and fell down and like to shake my skin off my bones with the sound. The window panes busted, and there was a funny, thin sort of blasty wind what zoomed through everything. Then everything was calm again. I opened my eyes a peek and took a look. Everything was like always, and I couldn't see no Devil or Hell. Out on the river I saw that one of the steamboats had blowed itself up. There was a fire, and remains all over the sandbar and on the shore were hunks of wood and such. Now comes the important part. Just then I turned around and there in the street come up from the river, with his clothes drippy wet, was that Guinea Sam man. He was one of them little bitty dried up men and he walked with a long, crooked, twisty cane and had big gold earrings and the blackest eyes I ever did see, sharp and mean and he looked right through you. He comes straight up to me and said "Sister, beware." "Mister," I said, "I'm so scared right now I couldn't do nothing if I wanted to." He said, "I'm a conjure man and I'm telling you right now that I've come to stay and there's a new day coming for this town." So he went down the street and I went in my house. There ain't no way of telling this—that conjure man came over here in a cannon ball just like he always said, and it was mis-aimed and landed on the boat in the river and busted it up. And there was a great change in Boonville from that day hereafter, just like that man said.

Sam himself added a few details for interviewers. He claimed to have been blown over from Africa in a cannonball, heading for Boonville. But the shot came up short, and he landed on a steamboat in the Missouri River. The boat exploded, but Sam stepped ashore, unharmed.

However it was that Sam arrived in Boonville, he became the strongest of the conjurers. Conjure men and women might be seers or healers; they might be known for their ability to curse or remove a curse from someone. They used charms, spells and materials, such as grave dust, herbs and animals, to ensure their magic was successful. Conjurers might also be called "heady," since they were so full of knowledge, or sometimes "two headed" men because they understood both the real and spirit worlds. Conjure men lived throughout Missouri in the nineteenth century, and it was not unusual for one "doctor" to be known as another's enemy and to become adept at removing his spells. Some conjure men had the ability to make themselves invisible or to command the natural world. Others could "fix" someone with a spell meant to teach the victim a lesson. A conjure man from outside St. Louis, Uncle Dinkie, wore a snakeskin around his neck and carried a dried frog and lizard. Although a slave, he was left to his own devices by the overseer on the plantation. It seems that one day Dinkie was to be flogged, and he asked the devil for help. When the overseer came into the barn with his whip, Dinkie showed him the devil and hell, and the man was so frightened, he never went near Dinkie again.

The conjure man calls on the spirit world for help. He can "lay on" love spells and curses, cure disease and appear and disappear into thin air. Guinea Sam claimed he had lived with a southern Indian tribe for several years, learning their ways of magic and curing. He cured people by making them throw up their evil, in the form of snakes or unearthly creatures—"a little three-jointed leggity, white thing which ran lippity, loppity across the floor."

Dr. Nightengale, as he preferred to be called, lived in a house located in the Spring Street alley of Boonville. He always wore a cross of wire around his neck and a good suit when everyone else wore overalls. He married a local woman and set up shop along Main Street. He was known all over the Boonslick for his skills in putting on and taking off curses, for throwing his own spells over someone and for calling on the invisible world for help.

One cold day in the river bottoms near Boonville, a group of slaves were out chopping wood. The men knew that if they stopped chopping and took time out to start a fire, the overseer would see the smoke and tie them to the "wild horse"—the whipping post—where he would teach them a brutal lesson. Hours went by until the men could not feel their frozen feet or hands, and still they chopped wood. They started singing hymns to take their minds off the misery of work, when suddenly they heard a voice: "Lay down those axes." The men looked around, and one said it was the wind. Then the voice came again: "Lay down those axes." The men were now too frightened to do anything.

Near this back alley lived Sam Nightengale, the hoodoo master of Boonville. *Image by M. Barile.*

Just then, out of thin air, appeared Sam Nightengale. He bellowed, "I said lay down those axes," and the men did as they were told. Slowly, the axes rose into the air by themselves and then flew over to the trees, where they began chopping away like one hundred men. Sam told the frightened men to build a fire, and he was then gone, as suddenly as he had appeared.

Sam could also command the elements. Uncle Henry of Fayette, a black storyteller who told stories of Guinea Sam, recalled his own meeting with the conjurer. Henry's family lived in an old brick house outside Glasgow, Missouri. One hot summer's day, Guinea Sam came up the walk and asked Henry's mother for food and lodging. Thinking Sam was a no-good tramp, she turned him away, and Sam called out, "Woman, you better think twice. People what knows me never turns me out."

"Then you had better go see them," snapped Henry's ma.

Sam waved his cane at her and warned, "Beware. Before night you will be driven from this house." And he left by the garden gate.

Henry continued:

About two hours later everything got still. The leaves just rested on the stems, and the birds just folded up their wings like they thought it was night. A cloud about the size of your hand moved over the sun, and then grew and grew until the sky was just like night. I got scared and ran inside. Then, when Ma and me was standing looking out the window at the clouds, a great big ball of fire rolled through the gate, down the path. Ma grabbed me and ran for the closet. The ball of fire rolled into the front door, and

Sam Nightengale was buried in Boonville's old Methodist cemetery (now Sunset Hills), established in 1835. *Image by M. Barile.*

started to nose around the room like a live thing, looking for us. Ma knew
it was after us for sure, so she threw open the closet door, and dragging me
behind her, ran around the fire and out into the yard. As soon as we were
outside and way down into the yard, we hard a big explosion, and then the
sun came back and it was like day again. Pa came running home, and none
of us wanted to go back in, so we slept outside for the night. The next day,
we went in the house, and everything was fine, except for a scorch mark on
the closet door. It was just like Sam told us.

When Sam died of old age, a local paper in Boonville offered a sketch of
his life and noted that he was buried in Sunset Hills Cemetery.

To the people who knew Sam, his burial was hardly permanent, and it
certainly wasn't what really happened. It seems that Sam got into a conjure
match with a heady woman from St. Louis. He was defeated and was carried
away in a cloud of smoke. But he "ain't dead yet," said those who knew him.
"He's liable to come back most any time and kick up a ruckus again." His
alley is still there in Boonville, and some folks are still waiting.

3

THE SPECTRAL GAMBLER AND OTHER TALES

1812 TO THE CIVIL WAR

The Boonslick frontier was a wild place no matter how or when you looked at it. In the early days of white immigration, the prairies were infested with biting, blood-sucking, green-headed flies, which could weaken the strongest horse and sicken the rider. There was no security for settlers, either, who were open to attacks by Native Americans intent on protecting their land or by scallywags and thieves intent on lining their pockets. The fur traders, boatmen and soldiers who spent time at forts upriver from Boonville, hundreds of miles from St. Louis, were known for their drunken sprees and vicious brawls. Franklin, Missouri, built a jail solely to house the military ruffians who plagued the town with their weapons and fists. Duels were common and could be set off by unintended insult or too much whiskey. The land was lashed by tornadoes ("devil winds," the native peoples called them), blizzards and floods. If you survived the endemic malaria or outbreaks of cholera, then you might be murdered. The coroner records listed causes of death, including murder by axe, razor, hanging, poison and beatings. It's no wonder death was often an extravagant visitor to the region.

Perhaps few occurrences caused more hauntings and legends than did war, and the Boonslick had its share of conflicts, from the early clashes with Indians to the War of 1812 and the Civil War. Ghosts from those times still walk, but the stories associated with them are often forgotten and should be returned to their rightful place on the shelf of legend.

THE SOLDIER'S GRAVE

This is not a haunting but a haunting mystery of the grave. In 1816, a hunting party was on its way through the Boonslick near the Lamine River in present-day Blackwater, Missouri, when it came upon an old, abandoned encampment. The men discovered a "cache" mound, where furs or other bulky goods were buried until the owners could return and collect the items. Digging into the mound, the men made a grisly discovery: within was a 3´ by 5´ by 4´ log "cabin" covered with a mat made of rushes. The cabin held the body of a man dressed in the clothing of a British military officer, with a red coat, gold lace, a waistcoat and cotton trousers. He had been placed carefully on another rush mat, sitting up and leaning against the log wall with a gold-headed cane placed near him. When the men removed the officer's hat, they discovered that he had been scalped. No indication of his name or military association remained, although a gold button had the word "Philadelphia" molded into it.

Who was the soldier? Had he and his fellows been in an Indian camp, only to find themselves in a pitched battle? Was the soldier scalped after the battle and then buried carefully by his fellow soldiers, with all the honor due an officer? The men who found the body believed it to have been that of a British soldier, sent to negotiate with local tribes against the Americans during the War of 1812. But the careful burial reflected respect and even friendship for the corpse.

A year or so later, the hunters again passed the grave, only to find it opened and desecrated by wolves, the skeleton strewn about the area. Today, the Lamine River region is still dotted with ancient burial mounds and a sense that some other place and time still exists along with ours.

THE SPECTRAL GAMBLER

This story was written in the 1830s by Alphonso Wetmore, an army officer posted to the Boonslick, and is typical of the frontier's dark and gothic sense of humor.

> *At a small village, there was a lingerer, whose personal appearance and propensities fixed upon him the title "the spectre gambler." Disease had made such inroads on his attenuated frame, that the effort of throwing a*

Gambling was serious business in Missouri when a card cheat could be dispatched by a pistol shot, but frontier humor might take advantage of a player's concentration. *Courtesy State Historical Society of Missouri.*

card extorted a groan; and a gurgling laugh, when he swept off the coins before him, threw him into a convulsive cough, that almost rendered him speechless. He was exceedingly irritable in his gaming, and those who played with him occasionally merited and drew down upon themselves his bitterest maledictions. These wranglings at midnight, the jingling of coins and tumblers on the table, would at intervals arouse all the village dogs, whose howlings marred the slumbers of innocence, and broke the repose of toil-worn artisans. Such was the untiring passion of the gamester for play, that he gave to exhausted nature no repose. When he had tired out, he was accustomed to sink into slumber on a rude settee, where he might be observed in the morning, muttering curses on the cards, ill luck and the human family.

On one occasion the gambler was sitting nearly erect in an easy-chair at the table which had been the night before surrounded with a dissolute circle of associates. Opposite him sat a silent being in an overcoat, the collar pulled up to muffle his face. Half a dozen tumblers remained on the table. A pack of cards was scattered over the benches and floor, torn and soiled; a few cigars remained, and one of the candles was still faintly flickering in the socket. Soon, the gambler awoke. As he slowly and painfully lifted his eyelids, and stretched out his fingers to collect the scattered cards on the table, he exclaimed impatiently, "Partner, it's your deal; wake up, you pale-livered imp! and cut 'em! I'll deal for you if you are too drunk." Receiving no answer, the gamester stretched out his legs and kicked at his silent partner. Perceiving no signs of life the gambler became enraged, and yelled as he lifted his crutch, "You're playing possum, are ye? after fobbing my money all night! I'll tickle your catastrophe!" and, suiting the action to the threat, he struck at the silent man. Whereat, the silent man fell over, and his "head" rolled across the floor to reveal a grinning hollow brainless skull. The gambler leaped from his chair and was never seen again in the town. And the local jokester returned the skeleton to the doctor's office, with the skull replaced.

THE GHOST OF HAIL RIDGE SCHOOL

Not far off the modern interstate near Overton is a road called Hail Ridge. Today, it leads up to a golf course, but in the 1860s, it was a lonesome settlement. One night, a traveler was passing the old schoolhouse when his horse spooked at a white figure, which rose, moaning, from the ground, waved its arms, cried and screamed and then disappeared suddenly into the earth. Many hunters reported seeing the ghost, which frightened their dogs into retreat, and soon no one would travel the road after dark. Finally, a ghost hunter posse was formed by Boonville men, who rode out under a new moon to track and destroy the apparition. The posse approached the schoolhouse and waited. Suddenly, the ghost rose from the earth, screaming and waving its arms, rising to a magnificent twelve feet. The posse turned as one and rode back to the city, where the men sat at a tavern and had a number of drinks in order to calm their nerves.

The men noticed that John Rayle, who lived on College Hill, had not made it back to the tavern. Rayle was slight and tubercular, perhaps too weak to run from the ghost. Just before the posse was going to return to the schoolhouse to search for John, the man himself appeared, carrying a large bundle of cloth and wood. "You owe me a drink," he said. "Here's your ghost."

The bundle revealed itself to be a wooden frame with bedsheets attached. And two members of the posse finally came forward with their story: They had fashioned the "ghost" and set it into an empty cistern. A series of ropes made the ghost rise and fall, and the screams came from the conspirators, who had hidden themselves near the school. Although the mystery was solved, the ghost of Hail Ridge remained a legend for over a century.

THE GRAVEYARD HAUNT

Old Franklin is now gone, washed away by the Missouri River in the 1820s. The folks who lived there moved up to what they called New Franklin, which remains on the flats above the river. But of Old Franklin, only a marker and a field remind travelers that a bustling and lively town once thrived—a true ghost town.

The boys of Franklin were notorious for their practical jokes, which caused bad feelings among Boonville people, who were often the butt of the jokes. Mark Cole, son of Santa Fe trader Stephen Cole, decided one night to hide near a new grave in the Franklin cemetery and scare several young ladies walking home late at night. In those days, graves were often built up with wooden frames and "roofs" in order to keep animals from disturbing the burials. When Mark sat down on the top of a grave to wait for his victims, the grave began, ever so slowly, to shift and move. Suddenly the "roof" was thudding like all the demons of hell were trying to escape as a lupine howling came from beneath the ground. Mark didn't wait to find out what it was. He ran for home, only to discover later that his friends had discovered his plans and decided to turn the tables on him. Mark would never travel alone at night after that.

SNAKES IN THE GRASS

Among the most feared animal bites were those from snakes, and rattlesnakes were the most feared of all. Those in Missouri grew to tremendous size, struck without warning and killed their victims quickly from fear alone, if not from the effects of the poison. People believed snakes had special powers beyond the bite—that they were a kind of spirit that hypnotized the victim.

In 1839, a Mr. Willard of Boonville told his story to the *Western Emigrant* newspaper. As a boy of thirteen, he was sent to cut briers near the fencerow, where rattlers loved to sun themselves. Willard saw a large rattler, coiled and ready to strike. He didn't have a weapon with him, but he stood still and looked at the snake. Willard stated that as he watched the reptile, he saw swirling colors and forms take shape and then heard "the most melodious, captivating and enchanting" music. He felt himself being irresistibly drawn toward the reptile, when he recalled Indian stories about the rattler's powers of enchantment. The boy made an effort to pull himself away, which took all his might as his mind told him to stay, listen and watch.

"And I fully believe that in a few moments longer, it would have been wholly out of my power to make an exertion sufficient to get away," he said.

4

HEADLESS HORRORS

THE HEADLESS COBBLER

There is a place south of Jefferson City called Smallet Cave, where alongside the cavern runs a spring-fed stream. The people who settled in the region were sturdy and independent, unafraid of hard work and not given to fancies and faints. But even they had a ghost that seemed attached to the cave and the community and appeared enough times to convince folks that the hereafter might just be the here and now.

It was "dusky dark" on a hot summer's night in the 1920s, the time toward evening when there is neither light nor blackness, just shadows. According to a story recorded by a family member, a local woman, Mrs. Haden, and a friend were walking the creek path on their way to a neighbor's cabin, where they expected to sit with a dying woman. Suddenly, a figure stepped from the shadows alongside the path and began walking along the road in front of the women. As startled as they were, the two friends realized that the figure was that of a man with a Bible on his shoulder—and no head. The figure walked (silently, of course) past the terrified women, who ran on to the cabin, where they told their story and took some time to calm their nerves. (The family story goes on to say that later in the evening, Mrs. Haden was sitting outside taking air when she leaned the chair backward against the cabin. In a moment, the air was filled with shrieks and movement, and Mrs. Haden said she nearly died of fright, thinking it was the creature come to get her. But it was only a calf, sleeping in the shadows and frightened when Mrs. Haden leaned on its tail.)

The first recorded appearance by the cobbler was not the last time he would startle folks. Other witnesses reported sightings of the ghost, sometimes with a Bible and other times with shoes draped around his neck, but always headless. He was known to step in front of horse and riders and then float away, sending the terrified witnesses galloping for home. At least one time he was mounted on a fine horse and passed silently between two surprised farmers riding home from market.

Who was the cobbler? People in the community believed that he haunted the nearby cave, where the tapping of a hammer on nails could be heard coming from the darkness inside. While this could be attributed to dripping water, it did not explain why experienced hunting hounds refused to enter the cave or the reports of hunters who threw rocks at "some thing" just inside the cave and watched in terror as the rocks went right through the being. Other people reported seeing what they called a lantern light, bobbing along the ridges near the cave, but no sound of a plane or automobile was ever heard.

The headless haunt's identity is a mystery. There were Civil War bushwhackers and battles in the area, so it's thought that the cobbler was a victim who returns to his place of death. Whoever he is, in such a wild place as Smallet Cave, only a headless haunt can do justice to the setting.

The Headless Man

Part of the region along the Missouri River in Howard County was known for its isolation. Between the wilderness and wildness, many deaths occurred that were gruesome, but few were as frightening as this one.

It seems that a cabin-raising was going on one October, and the men from surrounding settlements had turned out to raise the roof, as well as a jug of whiskey. By the end of the day, the bonfires were burning low, the cabin was half-roofed and inebriation was the general rule. One ruffian made the mistake of insulting another man about his gal, and knives were drawn. The fight seemed to be nothing more than a drunken brawl, until one of the men took a swing with his knife and cut off his opponent's head, which rolled behind a log.

The audience, who had been cheering on the fight, froze in horror. What was worse, the body remained standing until a voice came from behind the log. "Hurry up, come here. Closer, this way!"

The body slowly made its way to the log, a bit unsteady on its feet but guided by the voice.

"Pick me up, now!" called the head.

Finally, the body leaned over, picked up the head and placed it back on the neck, twisting it into place.

"That's better," said the head, looking left and right as it adjusted itself.

No one moved as the now reconnected head and torso turned and walked away into the shadows. Then the party broke up in a wild dash for their horses and wagons. The next day, someone found the "murdered" man wandering the road along the river. He was stark, raving mad, and around his neck was a circular red gash.

Old Raw Head

The Civil War left many homes and settlements in tatters, not only from battles, but also from the depredations of gangs and raiders who walked a fine line between outlaw and defender. Murders, lynchings and executions were common, and the names of killers and victims were kept secret long after the war, until now they are forgotten. Perhaps these unknowns have not moved on after all, given the consistent reports of hauntings that occurred long after the war ended. A number of Missouri ghosts seem to claim certain families as their own, appearing over and again to the same folks, generations over.

The small town of Versailles, Missouri, was home to another headless phantom, known locally as old Raw Head. This headless specter would appear sitting on haystacks or standing in the middle of the road and stopped horses and wagons in their tracks. The ghost was able to scream, or call out words, even without a head, but few stayed around to determine what he was trying to say. At least one family passed down their story of seeing the ghost on their farm, but whether he had been murdered there or was returning to seek his grave was never determined.

The Headless Horse of Morgan Street

While headless ghosts have been known on many occasions to appear to the unwary, a headless horse is more unusual. Did the horse lose its head in a gruesome battle and now must search for it for eternity? Or is the horse ghost merely unable to manifest its full body to a viewer? Perhaps there is a third reason, as suggested by the Morgan Street horror.

Boonville, in the center of the Boonslick, was the site of the first land battle west of the Mississippi River during the Civil War. The town was also an important strategic landing along the Missouri River bluffs, and no fewer than three battles took place there, with control of Boonville moving from Yankee hands to Confederate and, finally, back into Yankee hands again. This part of the world was known as both the Boonslick and "Little Dixie" because of the preponderance of early immigrants from Southern states and, later, for the strength of Confederate support provided by inhabitants of the town. Among these was Mrs. Brant, who lived at 714 Morgan Street in a two-story, imposing brick house. It was only twenty-five feet in width but well over one hundred feet in length, with nearly all its windows on the front. She was described as an imposing woman with an odd sense of fashion; she always wore a red wig with her lovely gowns. But whatever her fashion sense, she was outspoken, quick thinking and a devoted friend.

One cold autumn evening during the Civil War, Mrs. Brant was alone with her maid, waiting for a visit from Confederate Major Claiborne. Suddenly, Mrs. Brant's servant announced that a group of Union soldiers were at the door. The men told Mrs. Brant that they needed the house for the evening, and they expected dinner and her company. She ordered the servant to prepare dinner, and the officers asked her to remain with them for the meal. Mrs. Brant was trapped. She was afraid that any second the major would come walking up and be taken prisoner. Finally, the soldiers settled down for the night, but Mrs. Brant could not get out of the house.

She went up to her rooms on the third floor. There, she climbed out onto the side roof and, with skirts and cape billowing in the wind, edged her way to the top, grasped the chimney and carefully slid her way to the front of the house, where she braced against the decorative edging. She waited. She knew that if she called out a warning to Claiborne, the guards at the front door would waken in a moment. She knew that the mule barn near the house held both noisy mules and horses. Suddenly, her plan was complete. Mrs. Brant crouched there for what seemed like an hour until, down the street, she heard a group of people coming from a revival meeting. Right behind them was the major. As they approached the front of the house, Mrs. Brant pulled herself up and, with her cape clutched around her, whinnied like a horse. The group in the street saw the apparition, and several of them screamed. Mrs. Brant called out, "Run!" to the major. Without hesitating, he turned and ran down the alley to safety as the guards came clattering around the side of the house. In the hubbub, Mrs. Brant's hairpiece had detached and was returned to her in the morning by a silent Yankee officer.

Soon after, the rumor spread that Morgan Street was haunted by a headless horse with wings. The story frightened children for generations, until nearly a century later, a Brant family member revealed that the ghost was nothing more than the vision of a determined friend.

5

THE DEVIL'S FIDDLE

The Boonslick was a place where people shared their history and stories with as much gusto as they shared a meal with family and strangers alike. The French had explored the Boonslick region for furs in the eighteenth century and were familiar with western Illinois and the future state of Missouri. The Mississippi River may have been wide, but that did not stop settlers from visiting and trading among the Native American, Spanish and French villages. Among the latter was Cahokia, an eighteenth-century settlement built near ancient Native American burial mounds. The French may have settled in the wilderness, but they brought with them their old world traditions and enjoyed the celebrations of the year. (In fact, one poor community was known as Vide Poche—"empty pocket"—because of the people's enjoyment of life at the cost of their purse.) Ghosts still stalk the region, but sometimes the visitant has happier things in mind than a scare.

Just across the river from St. Louis, the village of Cahokia was known for its celebrations of Twelfth Night—the Epiphany—when the wise men were believed to have reached the manger and worshipped the Christ child. In Cahokia, thirteen bonfires were lighted in the town, a large fire representing the light of the world, and a small fire for Judas, which would be stamped out with passion by the celebrants. Singing and dancing went on through the night, and the music of the fiddle was especially prized. (After all, wasn't the fiddle called the devil's box because music might lead one into sin?) Finally, a special cake was served to the guests. The cake had charms baked into it, and each charm represented the finder's future: If one unwrapped a piece of cloth, he would be poor. If he unwrapped a coin, he would be wealthy

Twelfth Night was a time of celebration in the French settlements of the Mississippi River Valley. The holiday also marked the day when people ate, drank, assumed disguises and played other roles. A boy might become schoolteacher for a day, or the town loafer could be chosen mayor. But the mumming might also attract spirits of a different type. *Courtesy State Historical Society of Missouri.*

but was also expected to host the next year's dance. But the most important charm was the golden ring, which meant one was the king of the dance and entitled to choose his queen.

It was the mid-eighteenth century and Twelfth Night at Cahokia. Inside the log courthouse, where the dance would be held, Louison Florian waited with impatience for the music to begin. She was the pretty daughter of a wealthy tradesman, and he expected her to marry a man of great importance in the territory. Louison had little to say in the matter. She had given her heart to Beaurain, a good-natured scallawag with more heart than purse and a sword faster than a hummingbird's wing. Her father called Beaurain a cad, and refused to allow him in the house. Louison was brokenhearted, and Beaurain left the village in despair, although the gossips said he had merely moved on in search of easier conquests.

The driftwood collector Gwen Malhon was also in love with Louison, but he was an oaf and a boor, and Louison wanted nothing to do with him. Still, she had promised him a dance that evening if he could find a fiddler worthy of the party. Malhon knew that the boatmen might have a fiddler among them, so he set out for the river. Across the water came the strains of a lively French tune and the laughter of men. Malhon followed the shore until he came upon a raft tied up against the land. The men were dancing, laughing and drinking, and the fiddler was wrapped in a ragged cloak, but with magic in his fingertips. Malhon offered to pay well if the fiddler would come play at the dance. "I know a tune," cried the fiddler. "It's called 'Returned from the Grave,' and it makes everyone dance like they've never danced before." Malhon noticed that the man's face held glittering eyes, a pointed beard and dark hair curled about the ears. He walked with an odd limp, as if his feet were unused to land. For a moment, Malhon thought about returning without the fiddler, but a vision of an angry Louison ended this thought immediately. "We will pay well," promised Malhon. "I am certain you will," returned the stranger.

Before the dance began, Louison offered the fiddler a piece of Twelfth Night cake. She gave a little cry of surprise when the fiddler found the golden ring—he was now king of the festival and could choose his queen from among all the women. But instead, he picked up his fiddle, sat himself on a barrel and soon was playing tunes that could make the dead dance. Even the village priest threw aside his dislike of a good time and was kicking his heels with the rest of the village. The fiddler was the best they had ever heard, with one man shouting, "It is the Devil who plays—have the priest cool down the floor with holy water!"

Malhon watched Louison dance with every man but him, and when the fiddler smiled at her, Malhon had had enough. He rushed the fiddler, but before he reached his enemy, Malhon tripped and fell. At just that moment, the candles were snuffed, and from the dark came the voice of the fiddler, "By right of the ring the girl is mine." There followed a scream from Louison and the sound of a body tumbling, then shouts and cries. Finally, after a stick of wood had been lighted from the bonfire outside, the candles were relit, and the dancers saw an amazing sight. Malhon was stuffed headfirst into the barrel, kicking and yelling for help, his trousers sliced to shreds so he was baring all to the party. On the floor was a cloak, a beard and a fiddle, as if their owner had melted silently into the ground, leaving behind the scent of sulfur. But where was Louison?

The girl was gone, like dark before a flame. Louison's father fainted, but her mother was made of sterner stuff and beat Malhon until he led a search party into the wilderness for the lost girl. But all was to no avail. The devil, it seemed, had taken his bride.

Years later, rumors floated back to Cahokia that a beautiful woman and a scallywag with a fast sword were happily traveling the great river as actors. But Malhon never believed it. And to this day, Twelfth Night in Cahokia still has a cake with a ring, but also a blessing to keep away the devil.

6

BLUFF-TOP GHOSTS

THE BLACK CARRIAGE OF OVERTON LANDING AND THE LIGHT ON THE RIVER

THE BLACK CARRIAGE OF OVERTON LANDING

The roads to the old settlement of Overton Landing still wind and curve through narrow, tree-hung cuts down to the railroad track. Back then, the landing was a thriving Missouri River town connected to the east by ferryboat; now it is only the suggestion of a place where folks farmed and lived. Fred Oerly, the town's storyteller, soul and memory, recalled days when the landing was busy and his general store the meeting place for farmers, river men and lay-abouts. But Fred also recalled a darker period in the landing's history, when the dead rose from their graves and took to the back roads.

Overton Landing was a small, isolated farming community scattered along the bluffs and flats of the Missouri River near today's Interstate 70. As with many villages, everyone in Overton knew everyone else, helped out when needed, celebrated the harvest and passed along gossip. But not all Overton folks were community minded. One older couple lived along the river bluffs in a ramshackle wooden house just off the ferry path. The husband and wife had only each other and were unhappy about it—even if a kind person brought them some wood or a sack of apples, the couple took the gift without thanks or grace. They struggled to make ends meet and ran a tavern in their house, offering weary travelers food, drink and beds. But their unfriendly, sour and grasping nature affected the tavern's reputation and caused locals and travelers alike to avoid it. The couple remained apart in their own world as poverty gripped them like an unremitting fever, draining their souls as water drains into sand.

One stormy afternoon late in autumn, a merchant returning home after selling goods in St. Louis left the Overton steamboat landing and started on his way across country. But darkness came on fast, and just as the light was winking out, the man spied a faded sign that read, "Tavern." He stopped at the couple's door and asked to stay the night. The couple gave him the unheated back room—for a price, of course—and watched him check the time on a gold watch and then count out the payment from a purse fat with gold and silver. After he had gone to bed, the couple argued. Here was wealth, under their noses. All it would take was a blow or two. "I will do it for you," promised the man, "if it will make you happy." The wife did not say a word. But she slowly walked to the fireplace and handed her husband the cast-iron poker.

Later that night, the old couple struggled down the path with a blanket-wrapped bundle, dragging and heaving the deadweight along with curses and muffled grunts. Somehow, despite the wind and rain and their age, they reached the Missouri River and, with their last remnants of strength, shoved the burden into the water. They struggled back to the house in silence and cleaned and scrubbed the back room, leaving not a trace of the merchant. Once done, the man lavishly piled wood on the fire and burned the bedclothes—after all, he told his wife, now they could afford to have someone else chop the wood for them. They could have as much wood as they wanted for as long as they lived. But the husband was puzzled. He noticed that no matter how long he stood in front of the fire, he never got warm. First thing in the morning, I'll tear down the old chimney, he promised himself. Finally, the couple went to bed and slept dreamlessly for the first time in years.

After that night, the old couple changed. The community heard that a distant relative had left the man and wife an inheritance and watched as the couple built a new chimney, painted and repaired the rickety tavern and added a sweeping drive lined with trees and flowers. Everything they touched seemed to change to silver and gold, and the old man prospered in business as never before. They dressed to suit their new station in life, and the old woman's favorite gown was a rich, black crêpe. She traveled to church and back in a fine black carriage with a prancing horse, her husband always refusing to attend. Their new life was grand but short. After three years, the old woman suddenly took ill, and no one knew what was wrong or how to cure her. Neighbor women sat up with her night after night, until it was clear she was dying. She raved and cried about blood and an iron poker,

The twisty back roads near Overton Landing lead to the swampy river bottoms. Here, unwary travelers might follow the black carriage to their doom. *Courtesy Christine Montgomery.*

and the women tried to comfort her. Finally, the old woman, weakened to the point of death, motioned her husband to the bedside and begged him for one thing: "As I have stayed with you all my life, swear that you will never marry again." The old man felt affection for no one, but the old woman needed some peace, and he promised to remain alone through life. Night fell, and the old woman died, as peacefully as can be expected with the sin of murder on her conscience.

After a time, the man decided that with all his riches, he needed—no, he *deserved*—a wife. He courted a local widow, who was pretty, flighty and had nothing more on her mind than gowns and dances. They were married in St. Louis and returned home to Overton. The community heard news of their arrival, and some of the town jokers decided to give the couple a shivaree. By nightfall, dozens of men stood in the front yard of the couple's home, with torches and lanterns to light their way and pans, horns and bells to make a ruckus. The noise and shouting were overwhelming and brought the old man to the porch. His young wife stood in the doorway, terrified. "Get out of my yard!" the old man screamed. "Get out or I'll—"

The words froze in the evening air. The old man was speechless, staring out over the heads of the crowd. His silence stopped the visitors, who turned to look down the drive. There stood a black carriage with lanterns red as blood, drawn by a fine black horse and the coachman dressed in black with little of his face showing above his collar. But there was not a creak from the wheels or the springs, and the horse's hooves were completely silent. The crowd was hushed and stood aside as the carriage drew up to the porch before the old man. The coachman climbed down from his seat and slowly opened the door. The old man looked inside and then clutched his heart. There was the old woman in her black crêpe gown, staring straight ahead. Prodded by the coachman, the old man climbed into the carriage next to his dead spouse. The coachman shut the door, took the reins and started the carriage down the drive and into the darkness beyond. With a collective shout, the crowd ran for their lives, leaving the young bride staring into the night.

Nearly a century later, newspapers began to report weird experiences of travelers on their way to Overton Landing. Different people reported that while driving near the village, they nearly ran into "a funny old carriage, illuminated by two lamps and carrying an old couple in queer clothes." The accounts were consistent: the carriage appears only at night, on the back roads of Overton, and careens back and forth with no apparent fear of overturning or losing its way. The carriage is completely silent, and while it does not stop or acknowledge the presence of witnesses, it has been known to run cars off the road. The carriage is considered an ill omen and has nearly cost witnesses their lives. One man told of the night he was driving near Overton and was lost when a black carriage with lamps entered the road in front of the car. The man followed the carriage for a time and then realized with a shock that the river was only a few feet away. He braked just in time to avoid driving into the dark waters. "I thought the road was still safe," he reported to the interviewer. "I don't know where the carriage went."

Only a few years ago, a group of friends were driving through the area one summer night, car windows open and taking in the stars. Some of the roads in this area are unlighted, narrow and poorly marked, making driving slow. The driver saw ahead of her a dark vehicle and assumed that someone else was out enjoying a night's drive. By the time the driver rounded a bend, the vehicle was gone—probably, she thought, headed down one of the rutted side roads. Suddenly, one of the friends asked to stop. No sooner had the car slowed than the sound of a train blew through the hollow, and a Union Pacific locomotive and cars shot down the tracks—not a dozen feet in front of the car. The crossing was grade level and unlit, and the track was invisible until nearly upon it.

Overton Landing may be reached from I-70; follow the signs to the wildlife preserve. The Union Pacific railroad runs trains there daily, and the crossing is dangerous.

THE LIGHT ON THE RIVER

Ghosts are not just wispy phantoms of mist or ectoplasm. Sometimes they come in as many shapes and forms as they did when they were more substantially human. For, in addition to specters and apparitions, the idea of "ghostness" can also refer to the human spirit—or its disappearance. Folks still recall the house where this story occurred, but it has since fallen to neglect and ruin and spilled from its grand perch into the water far below the bluffs.

The Missouri River has always attracted adventurers and boatmen of a certain character—after all, the local saying was that "the boys go up the Mississippi, while the men go up the Missouri." Filled with snags and sawyers, the river claimed many a steamboat and raft and required a skilled pilot to maneuver ships through the dangerous shoals and backwaters in the

Steamboats coming up the Missouri would watch the bluffs near Arrow Rock for Mary's light, which she set in the window each night to guide her husband safely home. *Courtesy Christine Montgomery.*

dark of night. In the 1840s, such a man moved with his wife into their new home on the river bluffs near Arrow Rock. The couple's home was a cabin that had been added to and reshaped until it resembled a child's toy village. It was perched so close to the cliff that every window revealed the river. The young man worked on the steamboats as a pilot, and his wife cared for the house, which meant as much to her as did her husband. Every night, she would hang a lantern in the front window so that the wavering light would signal to her husband on the ship and guide him safely home. The other boatmen honored her tradition and called it "Mary's light," pointing it out to visitors and crews alike.

The couple was devoted, and Mary knew exactly when to expect her husband's return from the river. One time, however, he failed to climb the steep steps from the wharf. He had been downriver, so Mary didn't worry; his ship could have been held back by weather or a change in shipment schedules. But as the days turned into weeks, she grew frantic. No one at the levee knew where he had gone. Finally, Mary found a crew member who recalled that her husband was last seen in New Orleans. But where he went after that was a mystery. Mary was brokenhearted, but with no way to search and no one to turn to, she continued to live in the house, where she put the lantern in the window each night.

Twenty-five years passed, and the Civil War was raging when a ship's captain asked a member of his crew to pilot the steamboat upstream. It was a dangerous task, and the pilot had to know the river backwards and forwards. One weathered sailor was perfect. He knew the river, and he was very quiet; he didn't drink or play cards. He would do his best for the captain.

As the sailor guided the boat, he thought back on what little he could remember. He recalled waking up in a doctor's office in New Orleans, having been beaten by drunken ruffians and left for dead. His body soon healed, but his memory was gone. Inquiries led to no information—no one in the Crescent City knew who he was. And so he continued to do what he remembered in his arms, and eyes and ears—he worked on the steamboats, and now he was back on the Missouri.

As the ship steamed through a bend at Arrow Rock, the man saw the lantern. And everything, all the lost years and the lost memories, came flooding back. He landed the boat at a wood yard and left it to walk up the long hill. There was the cabin, and it looked as clean and crisp as ever. He knocked—and was soon looking at Mary's face. She stared at him. Who was this old man? He said he was her husband, but even he doubted it now. Who was this gray-haired woman with the vacant eyes? He tried to tell her what had happened, but she looked at him and said nothing. He remembered the young woman he had married, and there was nothing of her to be found in this lifeless soul. He touched her on the shoulder and then turned and left. Mary closed the door—it was turning to dusk—and went to put her lantern in the window.

The old Missouri is no more, leveed and channeled into submission by men intent on things being neat and tidy. But on a still, dark night, above the river at Arrow Rock, travelers say that a small yellow light sometimes gleams through the dark, floating above the ground—just at the height of a cabin window.

7

THE GHOST MUSIC OF
JOHN "BLIND" BOONE

John William Boone is known today primarily for his contributions to early ragtime music, but during his life he was among the most famous American pianists. He was a musical genius, a brilliant composer and a humanitarian, overcoming two major handicaps on his way to acclaim: he was blind since childhood, and he was black, the son of a former slave. His music is still performed at festivals and in concert halls today, although no recordings exist of Boone playing the piano. Still, his distinctive sound has not fully disappeared from memory, since at least two people have heard a most unusual "live" performance.

"Blind" Boone was born on May 17, 1864, in Missouri. His mother, Rachel Carpenter Hendricks, had been freed by Union troops and was a strong, smart woman, determined to provide her son with what he deserved in life. After the Civil War, Rachel moved with John to Warrensburg, married and worked as a housekeeper, even as her family grew. While still a toddler, John contracted a fever—perhaps meningitis—and was at the brink of death. One of the few ways to treat swelling caused by a brain fever was to remove the eyes, and Rachel listened to the doctors in order to save her son's life. John survived, but little was expected for his future. He was blind, poor and black at a time not long before Jim Crow laws would take full flight.

Even as a very young boy, John displayed a remarkable capacity for music. He would beat on pots and pans in intricate rhythms and make up songs and sing them to the neighborhood children while waiting for his mother to return home. Rachel worked for Senator Francis Cockrell, a politician

John Boone at the height of his fame. *Courtesy State Historical Society of Missouri.*

and former Civil War officer. Mrs. Cockrell took an interest in the young prodigy, and the town supported Rachel in her desire to send John to the school for the blind in St. Louis. John discovered the piano while at school and convinced an older student to give him lessons. It was soon clear that John was gifted. He was able to re-create any song or sound he heard once—and repeat it on the piano without errors. However, when a new school superintendent was appointed, he thought John would be better served learning to make brooms, and the boy ran away.

John returned home, became a street performer and eventually was taken under the wing of John Lange Jr., a black businessman and community leader. Lange and Boone's partnership resulted in fame and fortune for Boone, Lange believing that "merit, not sympathy, wins." Boone traveled the world but lived in a gracious frame house at 10 North Fourth Street, Columbia, in what was the Sharp End section, a traditionally black neighborhood.

Inside the house, Boone's piano had pride of place in the front parlor. He was a short man at five feet two, but powerful, especially when he played music, and he wore out sixteen pianos during his lifetime. Boone's last piano was a nine-foot grand Chickering—a huge, sturdy oak instrument with a cast-iron frame. It had a rich, unmistakable tone, and when Boone played, the sound carried through the house and out into the street where neighbors enjoyed impromptu concerts by their famous neighbor. Among Boone's compositions were a few that would later be called "ragtime," as well as classical "tone poems," which depicted through music everything from rainstorms to military battles and even animals.

Despite Boone's talent and fame, his career slowed drastically after the death of John Lange. Boone was facing the twentieth century, with its insistence on technology, speed and innovation, and his music—his imagination—had become old-fashioned in the public's mind. At his death in 1927, Boone was nearly bankrupt and left little to his wife's care, except the house and the piano. He was buried in a local cemetery, but there was no money for a headstone, so the world's greatest black musician rested in anonymity. But perhaps not in peace.

The beloved Chickering piano was still serviceable and was given to the Frederick Douglass School, which served the black community. For years, school assemblies and events were enlivened by songs played on the piano. Eventually, the piano was moved to the second floor of the school, where it accompanied music classes. In 1960, Naomi Jones, a Columbia resident, was interviewed by journalist and author Mary Paxton Keeley. During the conversation, Naomi was asked her opinion of John Boone. "Oh, nobody else ever played like Boone," she answered. Keeley was confused. Boone had died in 1927, when Naomi was barely old enough to remember his music, and there were no phonograph records of Boone. She asked Naomi when she had last heard Boone, and the stunning answer came, "Last winter." Naomi went on to explain that she and her daughter, Vickie, often walked by the school and listened in the twilight as Blind Boone played his beloved piano. "Vickie and me were going through the school grounds, about the time night was coming on, and when we were in front of the schoolhouse, Vickie stopped and said, 'What's that, Mamma?' I stood and listened—'That's Boone playing, Vickie,' and we stood there looking up at the dark windows where his piano stays, until he stopped playing." Naomi heard Boone on three separate occasions and could identify the ghostly songs, including ragtime and one of Boone's most technically difficult compositions, "The Marshfield Tornado." Naomi had no doubt that Boone's spirit was playing for her.

Naomi also knew that she had heard a ghost and that he wanted something from the living: a tombstone to mark

John "Blind" Boone loved his custom-made Chickering piano, which was reinforced with steel bars to withstand his powerful playing. The piano once played by a ghost is on display at the Boone County Historical Society in Columbia, Missouri. *Courtesy Boone County Historical Society.*

his grave. It was during this time that the Chickering piano was removed from the school for repair and then was used as the centerpiece of a fundraising campaign for the grave marker. However, the concert was a financial failure, and the piano was given to one of the organizers as security until he was paid.

Eventually, the piano ended up in storage, and later, when the organizer went bankrupt, the piano was sold by the bank to the Masonic Lodge of Pierce City, Missouri, for $864. There it remained until 1971, when it was rediscovered, purchased and returned to Columbia. Soon after that, Boone's grave and that of his wife, Eugenia, were finally graced by gravestones, nearly a half century after Boone's death.

And the piano played by a ghost? It can be seen at the local historical society, where ragtime performers stop by to pay homage to Boone and his music. Vickie is now a grandmother but still remembers clearly the night she heard music from the other side.

8

BOONE'S BONES AND OTHER TRAVELERS

I can't say as ever I was lost, but I was bewildered once for three days.
—Daniel Boone

Daniel Boone may be the classic American hero—self-sufficient, honest, brave and humble—but he is also a mystery. The ultimate frontiersman, he crossed the Cumberland Gap and opened the great American West to immigration, but he also earned the respect and friendship of some Native American leaders. The great symbol of Kentucky, Boone was born in Pennsylvania and met and married his wife, Rebecca, in North Carolina. He later migrated to Kentucky, where he worked as a surveyor and forager but was most famously known as a hunter and explorer. A man who loved being alone in the wilderness, Daniel lived near his ten children with Rebecca and scores of grandchildren. In his later years, Boone had few intentions of ever moving again, and when he died and was laid to rest, that seemed to be that. But the next world proved to be nearly as lively for Boone as this one.

Daniel Boone's last years were spent in Missouri in what was then Spanish territory. Back in Kentucky, he had been swindled out of land, and despite his great contributions, a corrupt state government refused to help the frontiersman regain his property. When Boone's sons decided to head north to Missouri, he began to talk about leaving a state that he now detested. The Spanish government heard of Boone's interest and realized that if Boone moved into the Louisiana Territory (which included present-day Missouri), then other emigrants would surely follow. So they offered him land and appointed him the syndic (judge) for the territory. In 1799, Boone and his family set out by flatboat and on foot. The Boones passed their first Missouri years in log homes near modern-day Defiance and Marthasville. There, Boone held court under the shade of large elms called "judgment trees," and he was respected for his fairness and honesty. Eventually Nathan Boone, the youngest of Daniel and Rebecca's children, built a limestone house on the property, and the extended family shared the home. Rebecca died in 1813 and was buried in a family "bury-ground." Her grave site was along Tuque Creek, near the village of Charette, and the burial ground itself was on top of a Native American mound that still rises from the farm fields. The shape of the mound may have given rise to the creek's name. "Tuque" means a close-fitting, rounded stocking cap worn by fur traders and mountain men. Daniel lived on for seven more years, well into his eighties, and was still active. One tradition says that he traveled hundreds of miles west on his long hunts after Rebecca's death. Then, in 1820, the elderly hunter developed a fever, and on September 26, he passed his last day among his family and friends and was buried next to Rebecca.

In 1845, Kentucky decided that the proper commemoration of its erstwhile son should include the moving and reinterment of Boone's remains to a magnificent burial spot overlooking the state capitol in Frankfort. Of course, Kentucky businessmen understood the publicity that would attend the transfer and hoped that once Boone was "home," he would draw in visitors to the grave site and presumably to the local taverns, inns and shops. The Kentuckians traveled to Missouri and approached Boone's granddaughters, who agreed to the move. According to tradition, the Kentuckians appeared at the graveyard located on the farm of Harvey Griswold (now on Monument Road in Marthasville). Griswold was angry and, defying the men, said that Boone had chosen his own grave site and should remain there. The men agreed to reimburse Griswold for any loss of income he might suffer in allowing the removal of Boone, and finally Griswold agreed. A large crowd gathered to watch the disinterment, which did not sit well with some Boone friends and family. One man commented that "Boone's bones…would have protested indignantly against their removal to Kentucky."

The work went on as three servants (possibly slaves) unearthed what remained of Boone. The men dug in the area indicated by family members and found bones, wood and fabric. Boone's coffin had deteriorated in the twenty years since his death, and there was nothing by which to clearly identify the body as his. In a gruesome sense of kinship, people reportedly picked up shards of bone and teeth to keep in memory of the great pathfinder.

Daniel Boone loved Missouri and expected that it would be his final resting place, but Kentucky had other ideas. This portrait was painted not long before his death and shows his hunting hat, which was not the coonskin cap of legend. *Courtesy State Historical Society of Missouri.*

The remains of Boone and Rebecca were transported to Kentucky by wagon, where they were reburied with great pomp and circumstance. Back in Missouri, the original graves were left open to the elements, and soon the gravestones toppled over, a sad reminder of Boone's absence. (They may now be seen at the Central Methodist University museum.) Not very long after the Boones had "moved" to Kentucky, the rumors started to circulate about who was really buried under the tall, marble Kentucky monument. Over a year, the story emerged that when Boone died, the family had planned to bury him beside Rebecca, but when the gravediggers began their work, they found that the grave site next to Rebecca had already been used. So instead of placing Boone next to Rebecca, they placed him near her feet. The family, unaware or uncaring of the change, raised the tombstones where they would

Daniel and Rebecca Boone were laid to rest on top of an Indian mound, but exactly where remains a mystery. *Courtesy State Historical Society of Missouri.*

have been if things had gone well—one at the head of Rebecca's grave and one at the head of the stranger's grave. Clearly, while the Kentuckians had located and moved Rebecca, they had not located Daniel's remains—only those of an unknown stranger. Daniel, therefore, may still rest alone along Tuque Creek in Missouri.

Today, the burial ground remains on private property but is open for public visits and still rises from the river bottoms, forming a platform above the stream. There are gravestones, interpretive signs and other evidence of modern interest, although on a bright autumn afternoon, when the place is alive with squirrels, and black walnuts and persimmons dot the ground, the peace is otherworldly. It is when twilight comes on that the cemetery and the road grow quiet and time seems to stop, and the shadows thicken into something else. Newspapers dating from the late nineteenth century reported that people often saw lights bobbing through the cemetery and around the graves, and despite the search for grave robbers or vandals, no one was ever found.

Older residents in the area reported the lights as late as the 1990s, when one gentleman described:

> *I was standing alongside the road, had been taking a walk. It was just after dusk. I looked up and saw lights. I wasn't that far away from them, but something kept me from climbing up to the graves. The lights weren't large, and they looked liked old-fashioned lamps, those old bulls-eye lamps. I could see the*

lights really clear—they would move over the graves, and then stop, like they was looking for something. But what got me going was the lights were above the ground, and I couldn't see no one holding them there. No one. I couldn't hear a thing neither, and finally, the lights just went out. And I went home.

The lights were too big for fireflies and too regular in movement for foxfire. Another witness told virtually the same story: She was driving near the mound and from a distance saw lights bobbing on top, as if someone were carrying a light or a lantern. She parked the car, but by the time she found a flashlight and got up the stairs, no one—or "no thing"—was there.

Like other ghost lights, the Tuque Creek mound lights seem to move with reason, and they have been seen for more than a century. Who is carrying them? The mound itself may date from as early as AD 1100, so perhaps the spirits of the builders have returned to check on their families. Or is Daniel seeking Rebecca, who is now a long, long way and time from his side?

A Trip Through Hell

When ghosts appear to the living, the occasions are often unexpected and uncontrollable. Yet among the ancient traditions found in Missouri was the belief that a spirit could be summoned through ritual. Parts of the Boonslick and the Ozarks were settled by people from Ireland and Scotland, countries with long histories of belief in the other world, spirits and ghosts. These settlers brought their traditions with them, and the rituals lived on in the backcountry hollows and settlements. There were charms for luck, for money and for health, and since marriage was an important milestone in a woman's life, it is not surprising that there were methods for trying to see one's destiny and future husband. This might be done by counting games or by interpreting dreams, but there was also a way to summon the knowledge through the ritual called a dumb, or silent, supper.

Dumb suppers were held at home and were generally most powerful during the days leading up to Halloween, when the barriers between real and spirit life were weakened. Conservative families often did not allow their daughters to participate in dumb suppers, calling the activity a form of witchcraft, but girls will be girls. One of the more frightening dumb suppers in Missouri, south of the Boonslick, was related in 1934 by a woman who recalled her experience firsthand to the folklorist Vance Randolph.

One autumn evening in 1900, two sisters were left at home while their parents visited relatives some distance away. The girls had invited friends to stay over for company, and as dark came on, the group decided to act out a dumb supper. In order for the supper to work properly, the participants had to strictly obey a series of rules. First, a simple supper of cornmeal and water was prepared and the table set—but the girls had to walk backward, set the table backward and do the work in complete silence. Once this was completed, the girls would stand behind the chairs, bow their heads and wait in silence. If all went well, at midnight the spirit of the girls' future husbands would be compelled to appear and sit in the chair. No words were to be spoken to them, and since it was believed that these spirits could not answer, the "dumb," or silent, part of the supper would be maintained.

Only one of the girls completed the "supper," since the others had become frightened as night came on and the candles were lit. They watched closely as the ritual drew on. The friends were surprised when the brave girl laid an unusual knife with a deer antler handle next to the plate, since everyday knives and forks were sufficient. The girls heard a storm approach, and the wind began to rise, whipping the trees back and forth against the sides of the cabin. Their friend completed her preparations and stood behind a chair, where she had carefully placed a plate, fork and the knife. As the clock chimed midnight, the door to the cabin suddenly blew open with a crash, and a dark figure walked in and sat at the table. The draft blew out the candles, and the girls screamed and scrambled for light. The kerosene lantern was finally lit, and all saw that the door was shut and the room empty—but the knife was gone from its place on the table. The hostess said she could not see the man's face, and all were thoroughly frightened and swore they would never hold a dumb supper again.

Several years later, the girl who had set the table married a man she met through family connections, and the happy couple set up housekeeping. According to one woman who had attended the dumb supper, her friend seemed to be content and in love with her husband. But one day, teasing her spouse about his height, the girl told the story of the dumb supper, noting that her husband was as tall as the stranger who sat at the table that night. The girl's husband listened in silence, then went to his suitcase and pulled out a knife—the same knife that had disappeared from the dumb supper table. The girl was terrified as her husband explained he had walked through hell that night, and it was her witchcraft that had forced him do so. He stabbed the girl and ran from the house, never to be seen again. The girl survived to tell the story, and friends, family and community believed her, knowing well that there are some things that cannot be explained.

THE SPOOK LIGHT OF CLARKS FORK

Southwestern Missouri is home to mysterious lights that have defied discovery and description for generations. Out Joplin way, the Hornet Spook Light dances and darts along Devil's Promenade Road, sometimes as a single white light, floating above cars and proving that science cannot explain everything. Near Smalletts Cave, the spook lights sail along a ridgeline above the trees. Although many theories for these luminescent visitations—including cars, will-o'-the-wisps and UFOs—have been offered, no theory has been accepted. But though the Hornet Spook Light is the most famous in Missouri, there are other, more mysterious lights that haunt the Boonslick. To date, no ghost hunter has captured images of the Clarks Fork spook light, an apparition that apparently knows its own mind and has for the past 170 years.

The small Boonslick settlement of Clarks Fork lies approximately seven miles south of Boonville in an isolated valley. The history of the area began with small settlements, and in the 1830s, a settler named Story built a cabin in what is now Clarks Fork Valley. He was a solitary man, one of those folks who kept to himself, raised his own crops and had few contacts with neighbors. Still, one day several men made a neighborly stop at the Story cabin, only to find the door open, the dogs wandering the yard and the fire cold. It appeared that nothing had been removed from the cabin; Story's rifle was there, as were his few belongings. Some folks believed he had just upped and left for the West, but others shook their heads. What man would leave behind his gun and dogs if he were going off to start a new life? Story's body was never found, and eventually the farm was sold to strangers. By the 1880s, a family named Houston was living on the Story farm. They had heard rumors of strange goings-on there and assumed it was local legend—nothing to worry about. But the Houstons soon learned that their quiet valley was haunted by a loud and busy ghost.

Living in Clarks Fork Valley was an entity called the Spook, which visited the valley every October and November. (Oddly enough, the word "spook," from an older word for "ghost," may be related to ancient beliefs in witches and will-o'-the-wisps, or glowing and moving lights.) The Houston family described the Spook as a ball of white light that would appear at night in snowstorms, rain or in the clear moonlight. The ball did not change size but floated above the trees or about the ground at waist height. It was always seen at the north valley rim. Sometimes it moved quickly; other times it might hover for more than an hour in a single spot, but it always finished

The Clarks Fork spook returned yearly to search for his old cabin in the backwoods of the fork. *Courtesy Tess Montgomery.*

up the night by floating to the Story cabin and hovering along each side for a few minutes, as if peering into remembered windows. Then it would drift down to the spring and finally float out of sight and into the dark.

The Spook seemed to enjoy company, at least on its own terms. Two families—the Wilsons and the Houstons—reported that when their dogs approached the light, the animals would stop, howl and back up, sometimes going to hide under the house. Even stranger, the Spook would come near the dogs, as if teasing them, but never harmed them. Missouri folklorist Charles Van Ravenswaay interviewed Houston descendants in the 1940s and learned that the Houston father and son once approached the light when it came up their farm road. The light followed the fence line and then stopped short of the house. Some nights, the Houston family would gather on the porch to watch the Spook's antics, and this time they decided to learn more. Father and son moved close enough to the ball of light to discover that it gave off no heat. But the duo noticed a dark shadow within the light, and extending from beneath the shadow were legs wrapped in old-fashioned buckskin. The family heard voices coming from the light and said it sounded as if a man and a boy were arguing, but they could not make out the words. Eventually, the light backed off and left for the evening.

The Spook certainly kept busy and enjoyed the routines of Missouri farm life. One family reportedly heard the Spook driving a herd of hogs through the forest. There were clear sounds of the Spook urging on the grunting and squealing animals, as well as loud snapping of branches and the rustling leaves as scores of hogs smashed through the forest. These were hardly sounds that could be mistaken for anything else, but not a trace was ever found by daylight of a hog drive the night before. The Spook also enjoyed hunting opossum each autumn. People heard the ghost approach and then listened as the hounds rushed through the woods. Next came the sound of an axe chopping a tree (where the real opossum presumably wondered what the heck was going on), the baying of the hounds and, finally, nothing. The next day, not a tree had been touched, and there was no evidence of the hunt. Mr. Houston recalled that as a child he would shiver in bed listening to the ghost calling and encouraging its hounds through the woods in a "voice" that called "Heeee!" running from a high register to low notes. It happened more than once, and Houston's memory of the Spook never dimmed. Other times, the Spook would whoosh around the valley, yelling and calling, and then fly up a tree, setting the branches ablaze with an intense white light. As usual, neither smoke nor burn damage was found by anyone the next day.

Sometimes the Spook would leave aside its work and play practical jokes on people. Once it stepped in front of a farmer's horse and wagon and frightened the horses into freezing in their tracks. As much as the farmer yelled and lashed the terrified animals, they stayed right there as the Spook hovered in front of them. Finally, the man's annoyed wife stood up in the wagon and began to sing a hymn, and in a moment, the Spook moved courteously aside, allowing the wagon to pass by. Another time, the Spook stood right in the middle of the road and stopped the horse of a fellow on his way to court a girl. The young man turned back in frustration, hightailing it for home.

No one ever identified the Spook or captured it on a recording. While Clarks Fork has more homes today than it did in the last century, there are still curving roads, open fields and dense underbrush enough to attract a ghost. And given the remoteness of the valley and the length of eternity, the Spook may certainly make a return visit this autumn or any other. After all, what is a century to someone—or something—with all the time in the next world?

9
HAUNTED FLORA AND FAUNA

From information we believe the late rise of the Missouri exceeds that of any
former period since the settlement of the country. Nearly all the islands were
inundated…During its rise an immense quantity of drift-wood floated on its
turbid bosom…and so filled up with other matter as to exhibit the appearance of
floating islands.
—Boonslick Advertiser

THE GHOST FLOWERS

John Hardeman of the Boonslick was, depending on whom one believes, an early Luther Burbank, a pirate who fled to Missouri in order to live in peace after his rambunctious life, a German emigrant, a French planter or an English farmer. In truth, he was born in Virginia and traveled with his family through the old Southwest, settling in Missouri. An attorney, antiquarian and agriculturist, John Hardeman was devoted to his family. He was also devoted to his farm until death.

Hardeman had come to Franklin from Tennessee and built a garden in the middle of the wilderness. He called his home Fruitage, several hundred acres along the Missouri near the present village of New Franklin. Hardeman was a farmer but wanted to do more than farm; he wanted to demonstrate that Missouri was as rich as any Eden in fruits, flowers and harvests. In the 1820s, Hardeman cleared approximately eleven acres at Fruitage and laid out a formal garden with a central maze, serpentine walks paved with crushed oyster shells, geometric patterns of planting beds, ponds and pools. To fill the garden, he imported fruits, trees, flowers and shrubs from around the world.

Letters to Hardeman show that he asked friends to collect seedlings and cuttings for his farm. George Sibley sent black and white grapes to Hardeman from Mexico in 1826 while on the Santa Fe survey, warning him to protect the vines from frosts and cold winter weather. Both on the farm and in the garden, Hardeman hoped to demonstrate the agricultural possibilities of the frontier. As part of his campaign, he published a letter to Missouri senator Thomas Hart Benton, praising the fertile land and the region. He joked that his Tennessee friends thought Missouri was too cold for cotton. But, he boasted, cold was useful: the devil once visited Missouri, caught a chill and never returned to beleaguer the state.

Hardeman was among those men and women who set up "experimental" farms, trying new methods of propagation as well as new crops. The Hardeman gardens were described by Missourians with something approaching awe that this could exist on the frontier:

> This spot of earth was adorned with fruit, and flowers, and trees, indigenous and exotic, with sombroso foliage, that lent enchantment to the labyrinth through which the serpentine paths led to the admiring visiter [sic]. Fruit-trees and ornamental shrubbery were transported, with successful care, more than a thousand miles, to perfect this favoured spot.

The fame of Hardeman's gardens drew many visitors, including Henry Shaw, who later founded the St. Louis Botanical Gardens. Hardeman knew that the Missouri flooded frequently, but he believed that a wide band of trees that surrounded Fruitage would serve as a levee and prevent the Missouri from flooding his land. Unfortunately, he was wrong, and much of his farm disappeared under the great floods of 1826 and 1827, although Hardeman continued to farm the remainder. The financial losses may have been one reason John became a Santa Fe trader in 1828, hoping that the trip "will enable me to spend the remainder of my days with my family." But it was not to be: once in Mexico, Hardeman traveled south and then boarded a ship for the return trip to New Orleans. Although he reached the Crescent City, he did not leave it. Hardeman died of yellow fever there in September 1829.

The family kept Fruitage for as long as possible, but eventually the farm passed into outside hands, and the land is now the site of the University of Missouri's Horticulture and Agroforestry Research Center (HARC). Since the change in ownership, no one has ever reported the ghost of John Hardeman returning to his farm—perhaps he finally found rest in a New Orleans graveyard. But something else returned, year after year.

For many years, a large rosebush bloomed along the banks of the Missouri River. It was visible from the river clinging to a forgotten corner of the old garden. No matter how much the river nibbled at the banks, or how many floods swallowed the land, still the rosebush bloomed each year, signaling summer to the upriver steamboats. It was also visible on land and was pointed out by passersby as the only survivor of Hardeman's gardens. Today, the river has changed mightily from Hardeman's time, but there are still reports by boaters of a red rosebush along the riverbanks below what was the old Hardeman property. A search from the land reveals nothing— but still the rosebush appears each June.

Nothing remains of Hardeman's gardens, but visitors are welcome at HARC during business hours.

THE SPIRIT OWL

Owls have always been symbols of mystery and the night. In some cultures, to hear an owl hoot meant death or that a witch was nearby, while in others, the owl brought fire to mankind or good luck to the harvest. The goddess Athena had an owl for a companion. Owls could see in the night and so were considered wise, since they could find the truth through the darkness. Missouri's owls include the barn owl, saw whet owl, barred owl and even the rare snowy owl, as well as others that hoot and call through the long summer nights. But none of them are as frightening as the owl that haunted a Missouri cabin along the river.

In the 1870s, a newspaper writer lived along the Kansas border with Missouri. He was considered an odd man, solitary, volatile and unfriendly. Eventually, he lost his job, but instead of moving to a city for work, he built a cabin on the Missouri side of the river. Although he had been fairly well known for his writing and articles, he had few friends. Despite his distrust of people, neighbors in the nearby village were friendly and thought he might be unbalanced, so once in awhile folks would drop in on the man to see that he had food and fuel. Things went on as usual, until the terrible day when a local family—husband, wife and children—was discovered murdered in their home. Only a small boy survived the massacre, and he was too traumatized to say anything. Soon after the funeral, the boy was sent to live with family members in Nebraska, and the crime remained unsolved. The community blamed a tramp or peddler, but no one was ever accused of the crime, and village life returned to normal.

Then one day a few years later, a youth returned to the community with a stunning accusation. He was the boy who had escaped the killings, and he identified the writer as the murderer. The sheriff and court did not know what to do since they had only the word of the youth; any evidence had been destroyed or lost years ago. But they were spared further action. Not long after the accusation was made, the youth disappeared. Suspicion grew that the writer had murdered the last witness to his earlier crime, but no proof existed with which to try him in court.

A few weeks after the young man went missing, the writer received the delivery of a cage containing a live owl. Attached was a note saying the owl was a favorite pet of the murdered family and was being sent to the writer by the missing youth. The writer was horrified and let the owl loose in the woods outside his cabin. Soon, the owl hooted all night long and stared in the window at the man, who in turn attempted to drive away the bird. No matter what the man did, the bird managed to find its way into the cabin and perched on the bed's footboard. The man would wake from a deep sleep and see the yellow eyes of the owl staring at him ceaselessly. According to the few people who knew him, the writer suffered from terrible dreams—of a woman in white with her head gashed open. She would walk into the room and pet the owl, and when the man woke in terror she would be gone. But the owl would still be there. Finally, the man succeeded in driving the owl from his cabin, killed the bird and buried it. But that night, he awoke to see the bird on his footboard, staring at him. The ghost of the murdered woman appeared slowly and then faded, and the man heard a voice command the owl to find and kill the devil in the man's heart so he might be set free. The man flung himself from his bed in terror and fled into the night.

The next day, he babbled about the ghost to some of the men in town, who went to examine the cabin. No evidence was found of an owl, alive or dead, and the man refused to enter his old home. The last thing anyone heard of him, he had moved to St. Louis, where he was known as an eccentric loner until his death years later.

10

Ravenswood and Rivercene

Ravenswood

A short drive south of Boonville, you come into the rolling Missouri farmland. Trees and brush push close to the road, creating shadows and sounds, and as you come around a turn, the fields open to reveal a Victorian fantasy of neo-Gothic gables, brick and wood. Massive white columns line the porch, and above stands a crenellated tower providing views of the surrounding countryside. The heavy wooden door is set deep into a red brick recess, a space filled with shadows where sunlight rarely touches. Light drops from a lantern high above the door. Billows of flowers and ferns spray from ancient urns, and there is a sense of time stopped between breaths. Around the farm, the woods press close, filled with shadows and the sound of birds—a place that embraces its name, Ravenswood.

The mansion and farm have been in the possession of the Leonard family since the 1820s. Nathaniel Leonard was from New York but had been lured west in search of adventure and success. His brother Abiel was a lawyer with a thriving practice in Fayette, Missouri, and a future in politics. Abiel partnered with Nathaniel in an eighty-acre tract of land outside Boonville, where Nathaniel built a log cabin, married and started a family, then began a successful mule trading business. A second home was destroyed by fire, and it was then that Nathaniel began to build a brick mansion, which reflected his success as a farmer, businessman and paterfamilias. He named the farm Ravenswood, after a character in Sir Walter Scott's 1819 gothic novel, *The Bride of Lammermoor*.

Gothic literature gloried in ghosts, death and decay, and many home builders added touches of the picturesque to their houses to give them a sense of age and tradition. Although Scott was a favorite author of Nathaniel, the selection of the Ravenswood name is odd. The story tells of the master of Ravenswood, who falls in love with an enemy's daughter. The marriage is thwarted and the daughter forced into a loveless match. Finally, the bride goes insane, kills her new husband on their wedding night and then takes her own life, while Ravenswood dies the next day in a pool of quicksand on the moors. Fortunately, the Leonard family would have a long and happy history at their Ravenswood.

Nathaniel died in 1876, after having completed only a portion of the mansion, and the work was taken up by his son. Charles Leonard was class valedictorian at the University of Missouri, served in the Civil War in support of the Union (even though his family owned slaves) and ever after was called "Captain." He fell in love with local belle Nadine Nelson, daughter of a wealthy Boonville banker. She grew up with great privilege and was friends with steamboat heiresses Cora and Alice Kinney (see Rivercene). Nadine, a slim, charming, dark-haired beauty, was known for her flirtatious ways and many admirers. The pet of her family, she was also a particular favorite of her father. When a child in 1861, she had recited a poem at school on the very day Union general Nathaniel Lyon marched troops into Boonville. Church bells were rung and guns fired to alert the city, but family diaries show that Nadine thought her papa had arranged the "celebration" in honor of her recitation.

Despite much competition for Nadine's attention, Charles eventually triumphed in the lists and married her. The young couple faced living in the still unfinished brick house at Ravenswood, so Charles's new father-in-law offered the young couple the choice of a house as a wedding gift. Local stories suggest that Nadine asked for Ravenswood, knowing full well that her doting father would miss her and eventually build her a house in town as well. And that he did. The house at Ravenswood was expanded several times over the years, eventually encompassing more than 200,000 bricks, wooden columns from an East Coast estate, mule and carriage barns and other outbuildings.

The Leonards lived up to their reputation for wealth and the social graces. The farm was the first in the world to breed shorthorn cattle, and the Ravenswood stock was sought after. The couple traveled the world, and Nadine—who had exquisite taste—filled Ravenswood with furniture and decorative items, including a sixteenth-century suit of Italian armor,

European bronzes, portraits by Missouri artist George Caleb Bingham, furniture from the 1904 World's Fair and much elaborate Victorian bric-a-brac. Her clothing came from the great design houses of Paris, including Worth's—magnificent froths of lace, beads and feathers, velvets, brocades and bustles. Charles and Nadine became famous for their lawn parties, lit by delicate Japanese lanterns and accompanied by orchestras and bands hired for the occasion. The powerful, the political and the local were invited and mingled under the Ravenswood trees.

One evening, after a dance, Nadine had retired to her room, only to be told by her maid that a nearby stream was over its banks and some guests were unable to leave. Ever the gracious hostess, Nadine returned downstairs and ordered the band to continue playing until morning and the servants to provide breakfast. Nadine loved family, friends and especially her home. She and Charles had one son, Nelson, and the Leonards continued to live and celebrate at Ravenswood.

Nadine died at the age of ninety at Ravenswood. According to the family, she passed away in her second-floor bedroom, which overlooks the sweeping front lawn of Ravenswood, the scene of so much society and elegance. After her death, Nadine's body was taken to Boonville for the funeral, but later that day, the family needed to retrieve some personal items from the bedroom. To their surprise, Nadine's door was shut—and locked from the inside. There was no way to accomplish this except with a key. Shaking the lock and pushing the door did no good. The family, worried about burglars, searched outside for evidence of footsteps and ladders, but nothing was found. For several days, they attempted to open the door, but with no success. Finally, Nelson ordered the servants to call a locksmith and remove the door, although this would result in damage to the woodwork. Before this could be done, a servant came to tell Nelson that the door had opened of its own accord. A search of the room revealed no intruders, and the lock was not latched. There was no reasonable explanation for this, except that Nadine had not wanted to leave her home, nor did she want her beloved Ravenswood marred in any way. The door was opened to another world—and apparently remains open.

Family members and visitors to Ravenswood continue to report ghostly happenings throughout the house and on the grounds. At the top of the grand staircase, just outside the master bedroom, is a small hallway table holding a music box. The box worked by placing a metal disk—somewhat resembling a rotary saw blade—on a turntable. The box was wound up, the disk spun and music floated out over the air. Nadine enjoyed the music—and still does.

Ravenswood is haunted by the spirit of Nadine Leonard, who lavished love and attention on her family and the house. This stairway leads to her room, where she has been known to lock the door and play her music box decades after her death. *Courtesy State Historical Society of Missouri.*

Visitors have reported hearing the music box creak to a start and play a tune, which would be odd enough on its own. But the gears are frozen in place, and the music box hasn't worked in many years. Not long after his mother's death, Nadine's son, Nelson, reported hearing strange sounds on the second floor and could never locate the source. Local people say that they hear music and see bobbing lights on the front lawn of Ravenswood, a shadow left, perhaps, by Nadine's parties and dances. Perhaps Nadine is not the only Leonard who still visits Ravenswood to make certain all is well. Nelson died in an auto accident on the property, crushed to death while opening the front gate when his car jumped out of gear. Some family members believe it might be Nelson who is the source of tapping and walking sounds sometimes heard downstairs in the house.

The current generation is working to restore the house, and they enjoy offering tours to visitors throughout the summer and autumn. It seems that no matter how many Leonards visit Ravenswood from the other world, they know they will find the seventh generation of the family still at home.

RIVERCENE

The most daring, the most resourceful, and the most successful of all the Missouri
River captains.
—Letter to a Boonville paper about Joseph Kinney

No one in the Boonslick ever knew when the Missouri River would rise from its bed to cover the land with a watery quilt of silt, trees and flotsam, so many people moved inland to avoid the floods. But James Kinney loved the river. He knew its waters, sloughs and currents. He faced it down in storm and darkness, but he always came back to it. When the time came to build his home, he couldn't part from the Missouri any more than a man could part from a lover. So Kinney did the only thing possible—he built his home literally right next to the river. Rivercene, he called the house and the estate. ("Cene" may have derived from an ancient word for "young girl.") The house is Second Empire–style Victorian; imposing, blocky and sure of itself and its worth. With its mansard roofs, six chimneys, rose color and porches facing river and field, to first glimpse Rivercene on a summer's evening from the deck of a steamboat must have been magical. It was the great house on the river, the finest in Missouri. (Later, the governor's home in Jefferson City would copy Rivercene's architecture.) In its day, Rivercene and its furnishings were worth $50,000 (an immense sum in the 1870s, when a family could manage on $1,000). Today, the house is still elegant, but visitors might experience more than lovely furnishings and fine food. It seems that the Kinneys can't bear to leave it.

Joseph Kinney was one of Missouri's most notable and highly successful steamboat men, with a career that spanned decades beginning in 1838 and continuing through the Civil War and into the early 1880s. His first business success as a shoe merchant enabled his full-time venture into steamboats. During his career, he built, captained and operated eleven steamboats, primarily on the Missouri and Mississippi Rivers. He was a tough but fair captain and a doting father who often docked at Rivercene so his daughters and their friends might enjoy a daylong frolic upriver. Kinney was a visionary and adventurer who championed the use of stern-wheeler steamboats on the Missouri River after he realized that a stern-wheeler was more maneuverable on the sandy, braided Missouri than a side-wheeler. He was ridiculed by many and refused insurance coverage by companies that feared the loss of goods if Kinney's stern-wheelers sank.

Kinney continued to ship goods and freight during the Civil War, one of the few captains who managed to do so. He retired from the river in 1869 and built Rivercene on five hundred acres across the Missouri River from Boonville. Kinney selected this site for the rich river bottomland (he was also a farmer) and for the fact that he did not have to pay the higher taxes charged by Boonville.

Kinney took many years to assemble the materials for his house, shipping fine woods like cypress and walnut, Italian marble and glass upriver to be stored on the property until his house could be built. There were eleven mantels of Italian marble and two walnut doors to the west parlor, weighing 250 pounds each. Rumors said there was a fishpond in the attic, although this was a zinc-lined tub for water collection, perhaps the first indoor plumbing system in the region. He knew that the river was always a threat to his home. The basement windows were set so that if the river overran the banks, the Missouri would flow through the basement from east to west, instead of pushing out the walls from north to south. Rivercene faced the river—so close that his neighbor's called it "Kinney's Folly"—so the Kinney steamboats could dock close at the front gate of the property. Kinney's plans worked well. Rivercene survived several major floods, including one where canoes floated and rescued people stranded on the second floor.

Nicknamed "Kinney's Folly" because it was built close to the Missouri River, Rivercene continues to haunt the landscape, as well as visitors. *Courtesy State Historical Society of Missouri.*

Ghosts, Ghouls and Monsters of Missouri's Heartland

Joseph Kinney died in 1892, and at age twenty-two, Noble, Joseph's youngest son, took over management of Rivercene. A student at the University of Missouri, Noble—according to one newspaper, "genial, popular and open-hearted"—began an expansion of the farm. He built a ninety- by sixty-foot greenhouse; planted berries, peas, tomatoes (reputed to be harvested by the first of May), cabbage, celery, radishes, pear orchards and potatoes; and rented land to farmers. Within two years, the farm was shipping produce throughout the Midwest and was gaining national fame. Then came disaster. Neighbors claimed Noble tripped and fell down the entrance stairs, breaking his neck. But his obituary states that he died of a "lingering disease" at the age of twenty-six.

After Noble's death, the Kinney mother and sisters were left to handle the estate. Alice Kinney (identified by locals as "a maiden daughter") apparently had much grit in her. As a girl, Alice had been seriously injured in a horse riding accident and could move about only with great effort and the help of a cane. She couldn't manage the whole farm, but she could manage the hothouse, and she raised a unique "crop" for several years: hothouse hogs. The family struggled to maintain the land and the home, and Alice and sister Cora remained at Rivercene until their deaths, but the house was sold out of the family in the 1960s.

Just when Rivercene began to be called a haunted house is unknown, but it seems that the house had a reputation for paranormal goings-on before the end of the nineteenth century. A local author, Lilburn Kingsbury, recalled that as a child in the 1890s,

> to reach the ferry we had to pass the Kinney mansion. I was curious about it as I had been told Captain Kinney had built, wonder of wonders, a fishpond in the attic. I felt uneasy, too, having heard it was haunted and restless spirits walked its spacious halls. From the moment it came into view until we had passed it, I never took my eyes off this great blue-gray house with rows of fig trees growing in tubs, which bordered its brick walks. Once past it, I had a feeling of relief at not having seen a spirit, mixed with disappointment at not having seen a living soul.

Kingsbury was born in 1883, so the ghost stories date to the time of Captain Kinney's death. Was the ghost of Captain Kinney returning to his home? A previous owner of the home described receiving playful shoves from out of thin air, tugs on clothing as if a child wanted attention and the distinct sound of voices in conversation when no one else was present. Some

Joseph Kinney, steamboat captain and builder of Rivercene, rests in Walnut Grove Cemetery with his wife and family nearby. *Courtesy Tess Montgomery.*

believe that Noble Kinney never left his home and returns to relive a happy and comfortable childhood.

Or perhaps something darker was occurring inside. Noble may have been a practical farmer, but his older brother, Joseph Jr., had more arcane interests. He was an odd man who, after his wife's death, sent his children to live with distant relatives while he remained at Rivercene. Joseph was fascinated by spiritualism and the thought that the living could communicate with the dead. He held séances in the house and practiced hypnotism on visitors, believing it to be a way to contact departed spirits. Servants were terrified to work at Rivercene, claiming that Joseph kept skulls in his room. (This may not have been as strange as it sounded. Joseph could have been merely a student of phrenology, the "science" of reading personality from the shape and texture of the skull, which was popular at the time.) Maids and groundskeepers reported to the community that they heard sounds of voices and footsteps and experienced objects moving from place to place inside Rivercene. Few wanted to be there after dark, and certainly never alone.

Modern-day visitors to Rivercene have reported objects moving from room to room, doors shutting and the sounds of invisible footsteps running up and down the great stairs. Of course, it is possible that Joseph's dabbling in séances opened the house to poltergeist activity. But whoever haunts Rivercene, the house is certainly a proper setting for all things paranormal.

11

BOO MIZZOU!

The University of Missouri was founded in 1839 in Columbia, after spirited competition from other Boonslick towns for the honor. As the first public university in what had been the Louisiana Purchase territory, MU—or "Mizzou"—is also the oldest public university west of the Mississippi River. The heart of the campus is the quadrangle, where red brick buildings and a group of stone columns call back the past for current students, who still gather there. The limestone columns are all that remain of Academic Hall, which burned in 1892. Legend says that ivy will not grow on one of the columns because a Civil War soldier was murdered there by a rival in love. The "quad" was the setting for a duel in 1853, when two students, William Wedderburn Thornton and Benjamin Franklin Handy, caned and shot at each other. One of the wounded men staggered to the stairs at Academic Hall, and the bloodstains he left could never be washed from the stone. The quad's history remains spooky into modern times. In the 1980s, two students reported seeing mist take shape and then move across campus. The students followed the mist but lost it in the maze of graves at the Columbia Cemetery on Broadway.

Not far from the quad, other buildings also offer a window into Mizzou's traditions, including the first homecoming game in the United States and the Fighting Tigers, a Civil War squadron that gave its name to the university sports teams. And while some universities may boast a resident ghost or two, Mizzou has several, dating back generations and all still spry and active. It seems that, like many alumni, the campus ghosts seem loath to leave old Mizzou. Their homecomings are eternal.

The University of Missouri quadrangle is the heart of the school, and alumni appear to return here even after death. *Photograph by M. Barile.*

THE RESIDENCE ON FRANCIS QUADRANGLE

The Chancellor's Residence, as it is now known, has been home to university presidents, chancellors and their families since 1867. Its warm red brick exterior is surrounded by gardens, where a life-size statue of Thomas Jefferson watches students from his bronze bench. Although the residence is now the oldest campus building, there was a still earlier house on the site, built in 1843. During the Civil War, hundreds of Union troops bivouacked on the MU campus, and the commanding officer lived in the original residence. (A local story states that Robert Todd, one of the first MU graduates, saved both Columbia and the university from torching by Union troops because his cousin, Mary, was married to Abraham Lincoln.)

The residence burned in 1865, only months after the end of the Civil War, due to a faulty flue, and it was not long after that the state government set aside $10,000 for a new home, which stands today. The first university president to live there was Daniel Read, who served from 1866 until 1876.

Read opened the university to women and was a popular educator. His family was equally well liked, and when a lake was added in front of the university buildings, it was named Lake St. Mary in honor of Read's daughter. Sadly, Read's wife, Alice, passed away at the residence in 1874, but it is not certain she ever left.

The first reports of ghostly sightings were recorded on April 3, 1890, in the *Columbia Missouri Herald* when a journalist described "eerie lights and shadowy figures waltzing in the house." The death of Alice Read was recalled, and a security detail was sent to keep an eye on the house. Perhaps some rambunctious students were playing practical jokes, but reports that the house was haunted continued to circulate.

Nearly a century after her death, Alice appears to remain in the house. Chancellor Emeritus Richard Wallace and his wife, Patricia, spent time there and experienced a number of strange events. "We often heard the grandfather clock chime, which would not be unusual, except it did not have a working mechanism." (And despite many attempts to repair the clock, it

The University of Missouri can boast of several ghosts, including those within the Chancellor's Residence. Reports seem to indicate that the attic is haunted by Alice Read, who died in the house. *Photograph by M. Barile.*

remains silent today.) There were frequent loud crashing sounds from the attic that had no clear cause, and objects were moved from one place to another or disappeared altogether. Everything was blamed on Alice, with one resident saying that Alice must not like electronic things since those are the first to disappear. But the haunting went beyond these occurrences, and few doubt that a spirit walks the residence.

"During the 1970s," recalls Dr. Wallace,

> *Patricia and I were not living in the residence, but I had my offices there, and we used the home for receptions and other events. One night, three friends—all, I might add, down to earth, practical and full of commonsense—decided to explore the house, because tradition said that Alice Read's spirit haunted the third floor. There was nothing much up there at the time: a few rooms, mostly unused. To the right of the stairs was a small space—it may have been a storage closet at one time. The three guests headed upstairs, and I was talking with other friends when we heard a commotion and met the explorers running downstairs. One told me, "You've got to close off the floor," and finally they calmed down enough to describe what had happened. It seems [that] as they walked down the hallway, they stopped at the door of a decorative grille, which closed off the hall from a storage space. One of them began to open the door—but all of a sudden, she heard a swishing sound, as of fabric, saw a flash of light and the door was pulled back out of her hand and shut. She tried again, and again it was pulled from her hand. Someone clearly did not want her to open the door. I headed upstairs to see what I might find, but when I got to the third floor, it was completely quiet. I checked everything, all the corners, windows, doors, and then examined the door [in question]. I opened and shut it. Whatever it was, the cause was something more than a passing car's headlights or a breeze. I've spent many evenings there working and generally left around 10:30 or 11:00 p.m. Most nights, it was quiet, and I didn't have a sense of anything out of place. But once in awhile, I would head upstairs to check the doors, faucets, lights, turning off things as I went downstairs. I would get to the bottom of the stairs, only to hear a door slam upstairs. I would head back up—and everything was as I had left it. I know that old houses have drafts, but this was a slam—something must have opened and shut the door with force. It didn't bother me very often, but at least one night, I heard the slam and then felt something wanted me to leave. And I did.*

Later residents of the home have described sounds, moving objects and a sense that someone is there in the house. One resident described an experience that rattled some family members:

> We had guests for one of the holidays, and one mom was sitting up with an ill child. Very late that night, the mother heard the elevator come to a stop, the alarm "bing" and the doors open, followed by the sound of steps. She assumed one of us was checking on someone. But no one was there. We had the elevator checked, but there was nothing wrong with it.

The usual explanation is that Alice Read is loath to leave her last home. "Children visit the house and ask where Alice lives. She must be a happy ghost, especially when the house is filled with family."

THE CONLEY HOUSE

Across campus from the residence is an 1868 Italianate brick house with floor-to-ceiling windows and a welcoming porch. Although once the Conley House, as it is known, stood on several acres, today it is part of the MU campus. Sanford F. Conley, the house's builder, was a well-to-do local businessman and banker, and his wife descended from a prominent Missouri family. Conley's unmarried sister, Sally, lived with the family and was known to be a sour, unpleasant woman. Conley family history says that as she was nearing death, Aunt Sally asked to be buried in the Conley House. The family agreed, although no one can say whether she was interred behind a wall or the parlor fireplace.

Like Alice Read, Aunt Sally is said to stay in the attic and comes downstairs only if the attic door is left open. When she does venture below, she floats about from room to room. One man who rented an apartment in the house reported waking up to see an old woman standing and staring at him while he slept. He managed to sleep after that by shutting the door, but he never forgot the encounter. The house is now used as office space, and Aunt Sally's portrait in the parlor still glares from its frame. The door to the attic is locked, but people often report the sense of being watched as they walk down the staircase, especially late in the evening. "I hold on to the banister when I'm leaving the house," says one office worker. "I just get this feeling that Aunt Sally might not be happy with me there—and there's no sense in taking chances."

But is it really Aunt Sally in the house? A short drive from the Conley House will bring you to the Columbia Cemetery on Broadway. Here are buried local luminaries, such as ragtime great John "Blind" Boone, Robert Todd and other leaders in Missouri's past. But a search among the gravestones will reveal a marker for "Sallie" F. Conley, who walked the earth from 1842 to 1918. Here is Aunt "Sallie's" final resting place—or is it? Is this grave a memorial to Sally's memory while her bones still rest in the walls of Conley House? Does her spirit remain in the attic watching over her home and any intruders? Or is there someone else who comes down from the attic to float through the rooms at night?

12
SPIRITED THEATERS

THESPIAN HALL

Perhaps theaters are among the most haunted buildings because of the emotions that emerge onstage. Not only do actors portray sadness, elation, jealousy and rage, but the audiences also contribute their feelings to the space. Theaters are filled with the characters and sounds of times past, and the traditions of theaters are old ones. Among them are the beliefs that all theaters have at least one ghost and that each performance night, theater people must leave a seat or two empty for the spirits to enjoy the play. Another spooky tradition is the "ghost light"—a single lamp carried onto the stage and left aglow each night. Although the most practical purpose is to keep stagehands from tripping over scenery and props, the lamp is also there for the comfort and safety of the resident ghosts. Of course, the older the theater, the more at home the ghosts, and Boonville, Missouri, has the oldest operating theater—Thespian Hall—in the American West.

Thespian Hall has been a theatrical landmark in Missouri since 1857, and even before it dominated the streetscape, the town was wild for drama. As early as 1838, the men of Boonville founded a thespian society—a drama club that produced plays for community entertainment. The society met and performed in a log cabin set on the river bluffs, the first such group west of the Mississippi River. Although none of the "actors" were professionals, the theater proved so popular that in 1855 the town voted to construct the present hall, which would house the theater, offices and a

Boonville's Thespian Hall is the oldest such structure still in use as a theater west of the Mississippi River. Built in 1857, the hall has served as a theater, library and offices, and during the Civil War it was a stable and field hospital. *Courtesy Friends of Historic Boonville.*

library. The Greek Revival building was built by slaves, and the bricks were burned at nearby kilns. The interior of Thespian Hall consisted of a stage area (this is the front part of the present building; the stage house was not added until years later), and on July 3, 1857, Thespian Hall opened with a grand ball and celebration.

The hall quickly became the center of social and dramatic entertainment in the town, but when the Civil War began, Thespian Hall was put to new uses. It is believed that horses were stabled inside the hall during the war and that some deaths occurred on site. The Second Battle of Boonville was fought along the street outside the hall, and wounded soldiers were brought to the steps or into the building, which was converted into a field hospital. One St. Louis newspaper claimed soldiers from the battle were treated based on their political associations. Boonville's many Confederate families preferred to help their own over Union soldiers. Later in the war, a military officer threatened to bombard the hall with cannon fire, but negotiations saved the grand building from total destruction.

After the war ended, the hall continued as a theater and presentation space for talks, dances and other events. A skating rink was once set up in the basement for the pleasure of local families. Traveling entertainers—including John "Blind" Boone—performed in the hall, attracting large crowds, but by the late 1890s there was talk of tearing down the "old" building. Instead, local businessmen remodeled the hall, adding a new stage house, slanting the floor for better sight lines to the stage and building the simple, elegant balcony and draped boxes. Still, tastes were changing quickly as the twentieth century neared, and within only a few years, Thespian Hall became a film palace, showing the new art of cinema. It again faced demolition in the 1960s, but the citizens of Boonville refused to let the hall be demolished and raised funds to restore the building. Today, it is open for shows, events and tours and remains a linchpin of the community.

Visitors to Thespian Hall may encounter more than other audience members. There is a resident bat, swooping down in chase of insects during concerts and adding to the gothic feel of the place. But there are also quieter, less visible visitors to the hall. Actors have reported seeing someone sitting in the audience during rehearsals. "I couldn't see his face," said an actor/director who worked in Thespian Hall numerous times. "But when I looked out from the stage, I could see a shadow, human shaped, sitting in the third row. It threw me the first time, and I left the stage to get a better look. Of course, he was gone. But back on stage, I could see him again. I didn't feel frightened. I remember hoping he wasn't the ghost of a critic."

Other people have reported hearing voices up in the catwalk, which can only be accessed by a vertigo-inducing ladder going straight up for two stories. The most common report about a ghost in Thespian Hall came from several actors: whoever is there is watching the show and doesn't seem to mean any harm. In fact, the spirit has been reported as bringing a sense of comradeship and encouragement, certainly not out of character for the actor of times past.

The basement of the hall is a different story, though. Low ceilinged and dark, it runs beneath the stage. Few people want to stay there more than a minute or two because there is a sense that one is not alone. "I was going downstairs to look for a prop," recalled a cast member from a troupe that re-created nineteenth-century plays.

At the bottom of the stairs, I stopped because for some reason I knew that a man was standing just inches away from me in the dark. I called out to one of the cast members, thinking he was pulling a not-so-funny stunt, but then I heard a movement to the side, a scrape like a shoe or boot hitting the floor, and a breath. It wasn't from above me—it was next to me. I was too shocked to turn on the light—and I knew that if I did, I would have to reach toward the sound. Suddenly, one of the actors called down looking for me, and I unfroze enough to turn on the light. There was no one else—that I could see. I've been in that cellar many times before that night, but this time I felt the presence of someone else. I can't say that it, he, was threatening, but that's the last time I go down there alone.

One man who worked at the theater was as skeptical as they come, but even he refused to go into the old reading room beneath the theater, especially into the dark corner, where, he said, "the spooks live." But there are pleasant visitors as well. A recent investigation of the theater by the Columbia Paranormal Society resulted in EVPs (electronic voice phenomena) of organ music, voices and whistling, as well as experiences with moving lights where no light existed. And in 2010, a Boonville native and singer with an international career recalled a concert she gave in Thespian Hall:

After the concert, I was gathering up my things from backstage, and my husband and son-in-law were onstage, taking photographs of the empty theater. A few days later, my son-in-law sent the photos by e-mail. There in the back row was a figure standing and listening. It is clearly a person; in fact, it was my mother, with the same style of clothing, an outline of her figure. My mother had died several years earlier. She lived in Boonville and enjoyed the shows at the hall, and she tried to come to all my concerts. Oddly enough, right before the show, I felt as if she was listening to me and enjoying the music. I loved to sing for her. When we saw the photo we were all stunned, but in a way, not surprised. We had more than six hundred people in the audience and a lot of local energy, so I guess Mom couldn't miss the concert after all.

When the photograph was shown to a local shop owner, she took one look at the picture and asked how long ago the picture was taken, noting that it "must have been eight years or more." Her husband was related to the woman in the photo, and they had played cards with her on numerous occasions. When told the photo was less than a year old, the shop owner went as silent as the grave.

Peter Pan Returns

To die will be an awfully big adventure.
—*J.M. Barrie,* Peter Pan

Stephens College opened in 1833 as the Columbia Female Academy and today is known for its Theater Department. But what the public rarely knows is that the department was founded by one of the most famous Broadway stage actresses, the lovely Maude Adams. Muse and friend of author and playwright J.M. Barrie, who wrote *Peter Pan*, Maude was most famous for her depiction of the boy who never grew up. Today, she is nearly forgotten, but less than a century ago, Adams inspired adoration from audiences and was the highest-paid actress in the United States. She divided the last years of her life between New York and Missouri and influenced many young actresses and artists. Although she died in 1953, she has never quite left the Stephens campus.

Maude was born in Salt Lake City, Utah, on November 11, 1872, to Annie Adams and James Kiskadden. Her maternal grandfather was a member of the early Church of Latter-day Saints, and her mother was a popular actress, a favorite of Mormon leader Brigham Young and his family. Maude's father was a banker and a Gentile, or non-Mormon, who had lived a wild life in the American West until settling down with a family. Annie and James married against her family's wishes, and she retired from the stage until after Maude's birth.

Maude debuted onstage at nine months of age in a comedy and then took a leave of absence from the stage for several years. She later gained notice as a natural child actor, but her father was not pleased and wanted her to leave the stage. Maude's mother, however, was tired of her husband's heavy drinking and decided to return to acting as a way to support herself and Maude. Maude received little formal education before the age of ten and left school at fourteen. In 1889, she became a protégé of New York impresario Charles Frohman. With her mother as her guardian and Frohman as her guide, Maude achieved immense popularity on New York's Broadway stages. Frohman and Maude worked closely together until his tragic death in 1915 on the *Lusitania*, which was sunk by a German submarine on the way to England. Frohman refused to take a lifeboat seat, preferring it go to women and children, and as he stood with friends, he quoted *Peter Pan*: "Why fear death? It is the most beautiful adventure in life." In minutes, he went down with the ship. (Frohman was rumored to have appeared at the moment of his death in his New York office, sitting at his desk. A clerk, surprised to see Mr. Frohman, was sent on his way by the ghost, who said he could not be helped. When the clerk returned with other employees, Frohman was gone and the office dark.)

Crushed by Frohman's death and family problems, Maude retired at the height of her beauty and popularity. She rarely appeared onstage, preferring to devote her time to developing the first color lighting system for film. Then, in 1935, President James Wood of Stephens College convinced Maude to come to Missouri as a professor of theater, a position that lasted until her death in 1953.

At Stephens, Maude was famous for her assignments of breathing and vocal exercises. It was not unusual during rehearsal weeks for a visitor to hear young women all over campus chanting, "Moo, mee, maaa," as part of their homework. Maude was a demanding taskmaster, believing that she was creating audiences and not actresses for the theater. She would spend long hours into the early morning working on the lighting and technical aspects of a play and was famous for imperiously summoning the technical staff to the stage at 2:00 a.m. for more work. Students and staff quickly learned to disappear when they heard her approach, her shoes making a distinct tapping sound across floors and sidewalk. Adams lived for a time in the President's House on campus, where she was treated like a queen and enjoyed ordering out-of-season strawberries for tea. Eccentric and brilliant, Maude was loved and respected by the students. She was most associated with campus buildings, including the old South Auditorium, which was torn down in 2004, and the President's House and Senior Hall (both of which still stand on campus). Stephens continues to honor Maude Adams with a permanent exhibit about her work and a national award named after her. Although Maude passed away nearly sixty years ago, her presence is still strong at Stephens, perhaps in more ways than one.

Some former students still remember Maude at Stephens, calling her imposing and aristocratic. "We were terrified of her," recalled one Stephens girl. "She would demand constant work and dedication, but she loved what she did and we knew that." The student also remembered a rather unusual encounter in the 1960s at Stephens:

> *I was in the auditorium, visiting the campus after several years away. It was evening, and I was waiting for a friend. Suddenly, across the floor, I heard those distinct footsteps—tap, tap, tap—and then heard Miss Adams's voice. I'm not certain what she was saying—I was too shocked to*

listen closely—but it was clear to me that she was teaching a class. That same repetition of nonsense syllables we always did. The sounds faded, and it was all quiet again, and I left pretty quickly, I can tell you.

Another former student reported seeing the figure of a short woman wrapped in a cloak:

I was on the campus one evening in the 1970s, having returned for an alumni event, and was walking near the President's House. I remember that the lights were on in the house, and I thought how lovely it looked. During my day on campus, it was a tradition for us to stop in at the house if the lights were on, and we were always welcomed by President Rainey and his family. As I looked that night, a figure walked up the front stairs to the door. It was a short woman, and she had on a funny little cap. I saw her standing there, at the door, and then she stepped to the side, and I didn't see her again. She didn't walk down the steps, and I did not see the door open. If people didn't think I was crazy, I would have said without a minute's hesitation that it was Miss Adams.

Other former students have reported hearing Maude speaking in South Auditorium, apparently reciting from Shakespeare or from *Chanticleer*, a play in which she starred on Broadway and, later, directed at Stephens. One woman who continued in theater after graduation said that every time she was onstage she felt that "Miss Adams was standing there with me. It wasn't wishful thinking—I just knew that she was making certain that I remembered all her breathing exercises." Apparently, Maude still watches over her students, even if from the next world.

13

GHOSTS IN THE PEN

Reader, behold this unfortunate youth as he sits in his lonely dungeon, his first day in the penitentiary. On a low chair, his elbows resting on his knees, his face buried in his hands, he sits and tries to imagine what is in store for him. He endeavors to peer into the future, and all is gloom. That sweet angel we call Hope, has spread her wings, taken her flight and left him comfortless. The cloud of despair, black as the Egyptian midnight, settles down upon him. He wishes that he was dead.
—*John N. Reynolds,* Twin Hells, *1890*

Missouri prisons held more than the dishonored, the debased and the convicted. It seems that even when you die, you cannot escape the confines of cell and bars. Nowhere is this more obvious than at the Missouri State Penitentiary (the Pen), in Jefferson City, where ghosts still flitter through the shadows and walk the halls in broad daylight.

The Missouri State Penitentiary—nicknamed "The Walls" for the extensive stone, brick and concrete fortifications surrounding the site—opened in 1836, the first U.S. prison built west of the Mississippi. To begin with, it was intended for only forty prisoners, among them horse thief Wilson Eidson, or Edson, who was the sole prisoner for several weeks. The original prison site was four acres, but over the next 168 years the penitentiary grew to forty-seven acres, a sprawling, limestone behemoth that housed some of the most violent convicts in the country. John N. Reynolds noted in *Twin Hells* (1890):

Few who entered the doors of the Missouri State Penitentiary in Jefferson City did so voluntarily. Other souls left involuntarily, courtesy of the gallows or gas chamber. But some people seem to have found a home here, even after death. *Photograph by M. Barile.*

> *The Missouri penitentiary is located in the southern suburbs of Jefferson City. Its entrance is from the north. It covers an area of seventeen acres. This tract of ground is surrounded by a stone wall twenty feet high and four feet thick. The prison enclosure is rectangular in form. At each of the four corners, and at stated intervals, towers arise eight feet, which are occupied by officers on duty.*

The prison population quickly outstripped the building's capacity, and more cellblocks were added. Early in its history, the prison was called a "school for rogues," a place known for its bloody uprisings, poor management and unenlightened methods of "rehabilitation." Prisoners were required to wear the ball and chain, were placed on limited bread and water diets as punishment and could be whipped by guards until they were near death. Witness the following nineteenth-century description by Reynolds of punishment for the most intractable prisoners:

This is one of the few penal institutions on our country where the cat-o-nine-tails is used. When a prisoner's conduct has been such that it is deemed advisable to whip him, he is taken from his cell and led to a post in the rear of one of the large buildings, out of sight of the other convicts. His clothing is then removed, with the exception of his shoes. These are left on his feet to catch the blood that flows down his limbs…he is tightly bound to a post with chains. Standing at the post, in a helpless condition, he receives the lash. The whip consists of several leather straps, or thongs, at the end of which small pieces of steel are fastened…After the punishment is over, the prisoner, half dead with fright and pain, is led back to his cell, where he remains for a day or two, that he may recuperate.

The prison was infamous for its riots, as well as for its inmates, among them James Earl Ray, Pretty Boy Floyd, Stagger Lee, Sonny Liston and Emma Goldman. Here was one of the bloodiest places to be incarcerated; cells were overcrowded, prisoners had weapons and assaults and murders were common. The Pen was also the location of the state's death chamber, where executions were carried out by cyanide gas, one of the more unpleasant ways to die by decree.

By the turn of the last century, the Pen was recognized as out of date, in badly decayed condition and inhumane. The prisoners were moved to a new facility in 2004 and the Pen shut. Some buildings were torn down, but many historical structures, including the gas chamber, were preserved from the wrecker's ball, although not from decay. Today, visitors can still get a sense of the grotesque conditions that existed at the prison in the past. And, if very lucky, they might also meet some of the Pen's prisoners, albeit in another form.

Few people give a thought to the female inmates of a prison such as the Missouri State Penitentiary, but they suffered as much, and probably more so, than the men. They worked for hours in terrible summer's heat or winter's cold, sewing or performing menial tasks with little heat and few fans. Many collapsed from the conditions. The women who were housed in H Hall were subject to frequent physical assaults by inmates and staff and had no recourse in the courts or elsewhere. At various times in the Pen's history, female prisoners were required to wear yellow and white dresses, striped prison "gowns" and, eventually, plain skirts and blouses in the style of the era. Kate Richard O'Hare was sent to the penitentiary for her antiwar work in 1919 and afterward became famous for her letters and protests against the brutality of the prison system. In one newspaper interview, it was noted that *perhaps the greatest improvement that Kate O'Hare brought about was in the treatment of women in the so-called "blind cell" or solitary confinement…*[here] *they were given a blanket and compelled to sleep on the cement floor. Once every 24 hours the victim was given a slice of bread and some water…O'Hare told the story of one of the convict women, Minnie Eddies, sent to the "blind cell" for 21 days, dying as the result of her experience there.*

Kate wrote in a letter home that there was so little religion in the prison, many inmates turned to the study of spiritualism and spent nights trying to contact their loved ones on the other side. Kate wrote to her husband:

Here in this grim cell house that battle between the old orthodoxy of the church, and the newer philosophy of [spiritualism] *is being waged, and the new is winning. These poor victims of society feel that God takes no concern for them and they are not strong enough to stand alone, so they find comfort for their sick souls in the belief that their dead comrades in misery come back to care for and protect them. In the weary hours after the lights are out the cell house is peopled by many ghosts, but they are all kindly, comfortable, amiable ghosts, who flit about all night on errands of mercy and love. There is one, more interesting than all the rest, more kindly and humane; some day I will write her story.*

Despite Kate's promise, no notes about the ghost or spirit appear in later writings. Who, or what, Kate was writing about is unknown. However, there is a ghost in the women's section called the Gray Lady that walks H Hall. Witnesses have described seeing a female figure dressed in a long skirt with a light-colored, high-collared blouse. The apparition walks past the women's cells on the bottom floor and has been heard along the upper cell walks high above, but it is not known whether she is one of the brutal prison matrons so vividly described by Kate or if the spirit is one of the kindly ghosts who still looks to aid a friend in need.

For a place of such misery, some of the ghosts at the prison seem quite humane and happy to be doing their jobs. Among these spirits is one dubbed "Fast Harry" by the staff. Marie Lacey, a guide for the prison ghost tours and member of the Jefferson City Paranormal Investigators, says this spirit has been seen several times by employees and appears to be as solid as the viewer. While closing up the site one evening, a tour manager was asked by a guide whether a man had finally left. The manager said that her head count showed that everyone had gone, but the guide insisted that a man dressed in a loose jacket and carrying a clipboard had passed her and walked quickly down one of the old walkways, a tunnel that connected the main prison to outer buildings. A search of the hallway revealed a locked door at the end and no other person. "Harry," it is thought, may be the spirit of a past "trusty"—a prisoner who has earned respect and responsibilities. Harry worked at the clinic, which was across the street from the prison, and among his jobs was to escort prisoners to and from the clinic through the tunnel. Apparently, even though he died far from the prison, Fast Harry has returned and continues to do his job with dedication.

Other apparitions are not so happy. One visitor saw the bloodied face of a prisoner looking out from the third tier of cells and asked to leave the tour. Later research showed that a man was murdered on that tier and died from blood loss after a fight. Other guides and visitors have reported hearing groans and cries near the death chamber.

Perhaps the most perplexing ghost story at the penitentiary, according to Lacey, took place in the summer of 2004, just before the prison was shut down. An inmate named John was waiting for the head count to be over when he spied a blond, long-haired inmate in a T-shirt and gray pants going outside for a smoke. John figured all was clear, and he followed the man into the yard. John was quickly stopped by a corrections officer, who said the head count was not finished and that John and the blond man had to return inside. John was happy to comply, but the other inmate was nowhere to be seen. The officer asked John the whereabouts of the other prisoner and then started to search the yard. No one in the security towers had seen anyone, and there was no exit along the fence. The now nervous officer checked inside a van parked in the yard, thinking that he might have an escape attempt on his hands. Then John commented that there were no inmates with long blond hair in that unit. The officer and John returned to the yard, and the inmate was never found.

Later, the officer told Marie, "I got goose bumps. It shook me. It's three in the afternoon, in a factory full of people, on a beautiful sunshiny day, and I'm outside running around looking for this thing." After the officer returned to the building, he appeared shaken and was asked by his manager what was wrong. "You're not going to believe this," replied the office, "but I just chased a ghost out of this place."

The Missouri State Penitentiary offers day and night tours and ghost hunts but is open by reservation only (www.missouripentours.com).

THE OLD COOPER COUNTY JAIL AND HANGING BARN

According to ghostly "rules," a spirit may be tied to a place because of unfinished business and the need to complete its work before moving from its old existence. It may repeat its actions again and again, hoping to get the living to pay attention and help it in some way, or it may react directly with the living in a conversation, as such. Apparently, ghosts can share their space with ghosts from other times, and the older the building, the more ghostly it can seem. So if any ghosts feel tied to the Boonslick, it may be those who still wander the halls of the Old Jail on Morgan Street in Boonville.

At first glance, the bulky, white limestone building appears to be a remnant of the nineteenth-century commercial district. But a closer look at the windows reveals heavy bars. And despite the lovely gardens which bloom each spring, scaffolds were once built in the jail yard for the execution of murderers. Today, the jail is open for tours. But who—or what—might a visitor expect to meet?

In 1848, slaves built the Old Jail of locally quarried limestone. The jail replaced an older log structure that was apparently somewhat easy to escape, if newspaper advertisements for the return of escapees are any indication. The Cooper County administrators spent $6,000 to build the jail, which remained in use until 1978, when it was ordered closed because of its poor conditions (defined by the courts of the time as "cruel and unusual punishment"). The original jail had only two rooms, in which criminals were shackled as they awaited trial and punishment. Ironically, the slaves who built the jail were also constructing their own cells because they were held in the jail, shackled to iron rings, until they were brought to auction at the market along a nearby street. During the Civil War, Boonville was a strategic river town; control of the bluffs meant control over the upriver Missouri. Possession of Boonville veered back and forth between the Yankees and Confederates, and the jail held prisoners from both sides.

The jail received a major renovation in 1871, when the sheriff's family quarters were added and new cells replaced the large holding rooms. The cells—called bullpens—were shipped to Boonville by steamboat, hauled by oxen to the site and then installed by workers, including the prisoners. The cells were heavy iron, with bunks, and were secured with padlocks. Between the cells and the windows, few prisoners would attempt escape, much less succeed in their efforts. Downstairs on the first floor was the holding cell for female prisoners and the execution cell, where condemned prisoners

The old Cooper County Jail was decommissioned in the 1970s, but apparently some spirits did not receive notice. The section just right of the door held slaves awaiting auction. *Courtesy Friends of Historic Boonville.*

awaited their appointment with the executioner. Frank James, brother of the murdered Jesse, was brought to the jail in 1884 to answer a warrant for a train robbery. The men of Boonville, believing that Frank was a good fellow, raised bond and took him out for some drinks (the case was later dismissed).

Executions were held in the yard of the prison, up against the south wall. Death was by hanging, and the events became public holidays, with people traveling from across the Boonslick to watch and enjoy a grisly carnival atmosphere. (At an earlier time, executions were held up the road at the old fort grounds, and the condemned was transferred by wagon as he sat on his own coffin.) The last public hanging took place in 1930, when young Lawrence Mabry was executed for murder, although this event occurred inside the barn, where the hanging drop door can still be seen. Eventually, public taste for macabre spectacle ended, and so did public executions.

After the jail closed, the structure was turned into offices for the Friends of Historic Boonville and is still open for tours. But few people want to stay there after dark, and fewer want to be there alone. The Friends are housed in the section of the jail that was home to the sheriff and his family, and a heavy door with a bar separates the two-story cell area from the offices.

Ghosts, Ghouls and Monsters of Missouri's Heartland

Through the years, visitors and workers have reported a number of strange encounters with unseen residents. "I was working in a back cell, looking for some papers. It was midday, but I had the lights on, since there are no windows on that side," recalled a director of the Friends organization.

> *Suddenly the lights went out and I was in pitch black darkness. I thought my sister, who was there helping in the office, was playing a joke on me, but I was pretty shaken up and felt my way to the door and then down the hall. I yelled at my sister—who, it appeared, hadn't left the office. Those lights have gone on and off like that a few times—but only when I'm working in one of the cells. We've had the wiring checked, had the switches repaired—everything is fine. But I'm not going into that cell alone ever again.*

Another visitor recalled that she knew someone was following her through the jail: "I stopped and turned around. No one. But when I took a few steps, there 'it' was again. I didn't feel threatened, but all the same—whatever was following me appeared to want to know why I was there."

In earlier days, the gallows were built as needed in the jail yard. Not seen in this photograph is the carriage barn, which also held a drop and noose. *Courtesy Friends of Historic Boonville.*

Workers at the jail report hearing loud moaning sounds and watching the lights flicker, and during a storm, there is no more active place for sounds: clangs, moans, creaks and whistles. "But I don't feel a negative presence," says Holly Peterson, executive director of the Friends.

Ghost hunters have visited the jail several times, and their experiences indicated the presence of at least one very active spirit. The Springfield (Missouri) Paranormal Research Group was in the upstairs cell area and received responses through magnetic field measurements and lights. "We asked if there was anyone with us, and the meters were completely dark. But the moment we asked if anyone present had served in the Civil War and was from Missouri, the lights blinked so hard, I thought they would pop," recalled one participant.

> *Later that night, I was in a cell, and asked whether anyone was with us because I was tired and wanted to finish up the night's work. The moment I asked the entities to show me something, my flashlight turned off. We were in pitch-black dark at that point, and we all jumped a bit. When I asked for additional proof that this was not a coincidence, the flashlight clicked back on. I'm not certain who it was, but he was teasing us, there was no doubt about it.*

The Old Cooper County Jail and Hanging Barn are open for tours. Call 660-882-7977 for more information.

14

SKYRIM

THE SORRAT GHOSTS

"As I sit here," Black Elk said after a long silence, "I can feel in this man beside me a strong desire to know the things of the Other World. He has been sent to learn what I know, and I will teach him."
—*John Neihardt,* Black Elk Speaks

North of the city of Columbia is a home called Skyrim, which describes well the view from the open, upland prairies of the region. In earlier days, the area was among the richest lands of the Boonslick and attracted settlers from Kentucky, the Carolinas, Arkansas and Virginia, giving the region its second nickname, "Little Dixie." More than a century later, one of the farms became home to John Gneisenau Neihardt (1881–1973), poet, teacher and author of the mystical classic *Black Elk Speaks*. Skyrim was a place of refuge and joy for the writer and his family, but few people today know the role that Skyrim played in Neihardt's avocation: paranormal researcher.

Neihardt was born in Illinois, moved to Kansas with his family as a young boy and grew to manhood in Nebraska. Once, as a child, Neihardt was ill with a fever and hallucinated that he was flying to get somewhere, as he wrote, "before it was too late, before the black curtain drops." This experience affected him so greatly that he believed he had been directed toward his life's work by an unseen being and knew that he was destined to become a writer and to explore the spiritual place of humankind in the world. He attended Teacher College, where he paid his way by working as the college bell ringer. Neihardt later became assistant to the Indian agent for the Omaha Reservation, and it was here that he began to gather stories about native life. His interviews with the Oglala holy man and shaman Black Elk, who was present at the Battle of Little Big Horn, became the basis for his *Black Elk Speaks*, a book of mystical visions, native history and personal courage that remains a bestseller. In his later years, Neihardt taught at the University of Missouri, where he was poet in residence and easily recognized on campus as the grand professor with a shock of white hair and an intense gaze.

Neihardt gained early fame as a writer and ethnographer and attracted the attention of artists, as well as readers. He wooed his future wife, Mona Martinsen, a wealthy, statuesque young woman, in an unusual way. She was a sculptress who studied with Auguste Rodin and had written to Neihardt that she had come under the spell of his writings. After corresponding for two years, John and Mona were engaged. They met for the first time in 1908 on the day before their wedding and remained passionately dedicated to each other throughout their lives. Neihardt continued writing and gained acclaim as a poet and author; in 1948, he accepted a faculty appointment at the University of Missouri. John and Mona purchased the farm, named it Skyrim and settled in with their children. Mona remained at Skyrim until her death in 1958 and John until 1968, when he moved to Lincoln, Nebraska (he died in Columbia in 1973).

John Neihardt apparently believed in other mind states from childhood onward. He recalled in a letter to family members:

> *I know that when I don't feel close to the "Other World" I'm miserable; and when I feel close, I feel invulnerable and can do anything I try to do. By "Other World" I don't know exactly what I mean; but it is probable that I mean a higher state of consciousness, at the least; and, at the most, an actual world of intelligences interpenetrating our world. The latter often seems the only thing to believe.*

Neihardt drew from mysticism in his poetry and from Native American beliefs, particularly those of the Sioux, with whom he spent time as both a writer and friend.

Among John's Missouri interests was the intriguing story of Patience Worth and Pearl Curran of St. Louis. In 1913, Curran, a young housewife, was using a Ouija board when she was contacted by an entity who identified herself as Patience Worth, a seventeenth-century Englishwoman. This was unusual enough, but what came after is still a mystery. Curran spent much

John Neihardt was intrigued by the mystic and spiritual all his life. He established the SORRAT research group in order to explore life after death. *Courtesy State Historical Society of Missouri.*

of her life taking dictation from the spirit and publishing Patience's work in books and poetry. Patience was lauded by reviewers as a gifted author, even if she was sending in her work from beyond the grave.

Neihardt was acquainted with two men who championed Worth and Curran: Carl Yost, a St. Louis newspaperman who promoted the spirit's writings, and Walter Franklin Prince, a scholar and psychical researcher who worked with Harry Houdini to debunk fake mediums. Prince—and Neihardt—both believed that Worth/Curran's writings were unexplainable unless they originated in the spirit world.

Neihardt and Mona were fascinated by the case, and soon their interest turned to active exploration in the form of séances at Skyrim. Neihardt knew that two of his students, John Thomas Richards and Joseph Mangini, were interested in telekinesis and spirit contact, and he invited them to sittings. By all descriptions, the séances were classic twentieth-century events, in which mediums fell into trances, cool breezes drifted in from nowhere and tables levitated and shook. Neihardt associated the round table work with the circle found in Sioux spiritualism and believed that Black Elk's spirit often returned and spoke through Mangini.

In 1961, Neihardt founded the Society for Research on Rapport and Telekinesis (SORRAT). He believed that group connections, or "rapport," were required for telekinesis—the movement of objects through thought. He also sought to explore out-of-body experiences, ESP and the connection between living minds and the dead. SORRAT had many members over the years, including Neihardt, Mona, Neihardt's daughter Alice, two granddaughters, other family members, students and friends. J.B. Rhine, an acquaintance of Neihardt, was convinced that the SORRAT research was an important source of information about extrasensory perception and life after death, and he sent a colleague, W. Cox, to attend the séances and report on the outcomes.

Photographs from the SORRAT studies recorded some unusual events, including a levitating doll, a moving table and other manifestations of spirit behaviors. One photo series shows a metal TV tray floating in air, and another tray is shown "walking" out the door and into the garden. Neihardt kept detailed notes of the activity. In a report from 1966, he wrote that he and two friends experienced a table's levitation. He wanted to test whether he was dealing with an intelligent entity manipulating the furniture, so he asked the table to bring him a book from his shelf. To John's astonishment, the table did so, and chose a book, according to Neihardt, about which he had been thinking but whose title he had not said aloud.

William Cox was so fascinated by the events at Skyrim that he eventually moved to Rolla, Missouri, and set up his own lab with funding provided by the McDonnell Institute for Psychical Research at Washington University in St. Louis. Cox invented a sealed glass minilab nicknamed the "Cox Box," filled with objects like pens, paper, sets of rings and other items. Cox believed the box provided researchers with a way of viewing the results of psychokinesis (the manipulation of objects by thought) without being accused of fraud. SORRAT and Neihardt embraced the new technique, and the meetings and experiments continued. Mona died in 1968 but returned frequently to SORRAT meetings and talked with John. After Neihardt's death in 1973, his spirit also contacted the SORRAT group. Whatever went on at Skyrim Ranch, John and Mona Neihardt's interest in the other world resulted in arguments among paranormal researchers that continue to this day. But it may be possible to ask John his intentions, for apparently he still returns to Columbia, Missouri.

Along the Boonslick Trail, above Perche Creek, is a house with ties to John Neihardt, for it was here that his daughter Hilda lived and here that he passed away in 1973. The family who currently owns the home purchased it from Hilda, and they believe that a Neihardt still visits occasionally and from a long distance. The owner describes unusual electrical events throughout the house. "We've had the electric service to the house checked many times when we were doing renovations. Everything always appears fine. But for years, lights in the house are turned on and off," she says. "In fact, while I was talking with a friend by phone and mentioned this interview, the lights went on. This has happened since we have owned the house, which we purchased in the 1970s."

The goings-on are not relegated to electrical happenings. One of the family's sons refuses to sleep in the guest bedroom because he has woken to see an older man with bushy hair standing there watching him. Anyone who has seen a portrait of Neihardt knows his hair was his pride and joy. "We know it is Neihardt," laughs the owner, "but nothing will get our son to stay in that room, and he's a grown man."

Others besides family have experienced things at the old house as well. John Neihardt's granddaughter Cora and the house's owner were riding along a bridle path on the property when Cora's horse shied. "I assumed the horse had seen something, but Cora assured me that it was only a spirit crossing the path," said the woman. "I believe that land can be home to spirits, and this land certainly seems to be."

Might John Neihardt have learned the skills of returning from the dead as taught by Patience Worth? Given that both were poets and authors, and both seemed to enjoy a Missouri visit, it very well could be an eternal question finally answered.

15

COME PLAY WITH ME IN MY GRAVE

THE GHOSTLY CHILD

Thomas T. Crittenden was a Kentucky native and lawyer who moved to Missouri in 1857. Despite Southern roots, his sympathies were with the Union, and he served in the Missouri State Militia. After the war, he entered politics and proved popular with the public, and by 1881, Crittenden had been elected governor of Missouri.

Among his goals was the end of banditry in the state at a time when the most famous bandits were outlaws, bank robbers and killers Frank and Jesse James. Crittenden convinced railroad executives to put up reward money for the capture—or death—of James Gang members. Rumors soon flew that Crittenden was targeted for assassination by the gang, and he assigned bodyguards to his family, which included Mrs. Crittenden, six sons and a daughter, Caroline. But eventually, the gang's "code of honor" cracked wide open. Robert Ford and his brother, who rode with the James boys, negotiated a deal with Crittenden, by which they would receive $10,000 for killing Jesse James. On April 3, 1882, Ford murdered Jesse James in St. Joseph, Missouri. Crittenden soon arrested, tried, condemned and pardoned the Fords. (The Fords did not receive the full reward.) With Jesse dead, Frank James turned himself in (and also received a pardon from Crittenden.) The James boys had finally been tamed, and Crittenden was credited with their defeat.

The Crittendens lived in the Missouri Governor's Mansion, which was built on the site of the original Missouri capitol. The mansion is an imposing

A savvy politician, Thomas Crittenden was hailed as a hero for bringing the James Gang to its end. But he couldn't stand between death and his daughter. *Courtesy State Historical Society of Missouri.*

brick building, with a mansard roof, decorative ironwork and a sense of its own history. The home is surrounded by formal gardens, pathways and fountains and offers a peaceful retreat from politics and the world.

But Crittenden had only months to celebrate his victory and popularity before tragedy visited his home. Daughter Caroline, born on October 8, 1873, was an especial favorite with the public, by all accounts a charming and happy child who loved playing on the grounds of the mansion. But despite the care and protection offered the girl, even bodyguards could not prevent an attack by a deadly assailant. Diphtheria, common among children, struck suddenly, causing breathing and heart complications. On December 20, 1882, Caroline died in the mansion. She was buried in Kansas City at the family plot in Forest Hill Cemetery, amid the grief of her family.

For more than a century, Caroline appeared to be at peace. But in the 1980s, during the term of Governor Kit Bond, the mansion underwent extensive renovations. One day, a workman who had been in the attic asked the housekeeper about the little girl. The man described her as playing upstairs near him all day. She was about nine years old, blond and very happy. Was she a family member? The housekeeper was stunned: the Bonds did not have a daughter, and as far as the woman knew, no children were visiting the mansion at the time. The workman insisted that the girl had been there all day. But when he finally realized that his new friend was less than corporeal, the man refused to return to the job.

One tradition at the mansion is that a sculpture of a girl at play on one of the garden fountains is a portrait of Caroline. Visitors to the mansion report sounds of footsteps going up and down the stairs, things moving about and other pranks dear to the hearts of children. It just might be possible that Caroline Crittenden returns to her playroom, where she is as happy now as she was more than a century ago.

AUNT ETERNITY

The Muir family was well known in Boonville, Cooper County, Missouri, having migrated there from Virginia in the early nineteenth century. They were lawyers, doctors and farmers, and their homes were substantial brick, solid and well to do, open to neighbors and travelers alike. But step around to the back, and one would find that the yard was ringed by small, rickety cabins to house the family slaves. Howard Thornton Muir owned house slaves and field hands, and it was these men and women who made it possible for the Muirs to raise tobacco, hemp, fruits and vegetables and to prosper beyond subsistence farming. The slaves were not encouraged to read, but if they did, the Bible was the only book allowed, since it showed slaves that the church's need for them was as good and faithful servants.

Muir and his family enjoyed the privileges of wealth and the society of other slave owners in Boonville. They visited among houses, held balls and celebrations and left their slaves to manage the farm. By all accounts, the Muir servants were dependable and skilled workers who kept their peace and attempted to avoid the whip of the overseer or the anger of the "master." Muir counted himself a fair owner and prided himself on treating his slaves well. But he had a terrible temper when angry, and many had felt the whip after a small infraction.

Not long before the Civil War thundered through Missouri, young Nancy Muir reached the age of courtship and looked forward to the picnics and dances planned by her parents over the next months. She traveled to St. Louis to select lovely materials for her gowns and returned with her family to Boonville by steamboat. But by the next day at home, Nancy woke with a high fever and chills. She had always been a healthy girl, and the family was not worried, until the fever worsened over the next days. Howard sent for local doctors, who did what they could for the girl, but they did not know what had sickened her. Sadly, Nancy died and was buried in the family cemetery across the road.

Howard Muir was devastated. Although death was a common companion in the 1850s, Howard could not accept that his healthy child was now gone. He brooded for weeks in his study, and the family feared that his sanity had been weakened by grief. The only way Howard could believe his daughter was gone was to believe that someone had caused her death. But who was it? The only people who hated him were the slaves, but he knew that none of them had the means to hurt him or his loved ones. Except, perhaps, for one: Aunt Eternity. She was born in the late eighteenth century and was brought to Virginia on a slave ship just after the American Revolution. As her children were sold away from her through the years, Aunt Eternity learned to hate and to nurse that hate carefully, as one did a smoldering log. The other slaves feared her, and she ruled the slave quarters.

Aunt Eternity knew how to mix herbs, flowers, roots and mushrooms into potions that could cure—or kill. Knowing this, Howard Muir decided that it must have been Aunt Eternity who killed Nancy with poison in revenge for her own children. His wife and children, doubting his sanity, tried to convince him that this could not be true. After all, none of them had taken ill, and they had eaten the same foods as Nancy. Despite the lack of evidence, Howard remained steadfast in his belief. One night—perhaps after drinking—Howard took a whip from the overseer's office and went to Aunt Eternity's cabin. The old woman was dozing in her rocking chair and woke to see Howard raise the whip as he screamed curses at her. As she called for help and mercy, Howard beat her again and again, and by the time he dropped the whip, Aunt Eternity was near death. The overseer and Mrs. Muir rushed to the cabin and there tended to Aunt Eternity, who, weak and broken, managed to croak out a curse: the Muir family would be destroyed and lose all they held dear. Howard Muir staggered back to the house and was later told that Aunt Eternity had died.

Eternity's curse took hold within a year after her death. According to local and family history, several Muir family members died unexpectedly; others died young, and Howard Muir descended into insanity after the night of the murder. The farm could not succeed without his guidance, and the land was sold out of the family. Although other Muir family members remained in the area (William Muir's home was still standing in the 1930s), Howard Muir's family left the Boonville region—all except one.

After the Muir home was abandoned, no one wanted to live among such sadness, and the house fell into ruin. Travelers reported seeing a light like a flickering candle moving from room to room through the deserted ruin, as if searching for something—or someone. The house is now gone, but the tiny cemetery remains. People have reported hearing someone singing near the burial ground, even as a search turned up nothing and no one. Others have reported seeing a young girl dressed in white standing alongside the road. The sightings occurred in early evening, but no one was ever able to reach the girl, who disappeared quickly into the shadows.

Searches of Missouri census and death records reveal no Howard Thornton or Nancy Muir; whoever they were, if they lived in the Boonslick, their stories have been wiped clean from the historical slate. There were

Muirs in Boonville, and they certainly owned slaves, but few records offer the names of these men and women, and no Eternity was identified. Records of the time show that Maria Muir's slaves left the farm as soon as they were allowed to enlist in the Union army. Whoever the girl in white may be, she remains a mystery. Perhaps she is Nancy Muir, hoping to find her family once again at home.

Help Wanted by Ghosts

Mike Shaw is a genealogist and historian from Warrensburg, Missouri, who was never quite sure about the existence of ghosts. Like many other people, he hoped for evidence but reserved judgment about the paranormal. When asked about ghosts for this book, he stopped and thought and finally said that one experience had caused him to rethink what is and what might be. Here is his story:

For several years, I commuted into Kansas City to work, a seventy-mile drive. Some days I drove our pickup truck, and on those days I would often take a shortcut to the highway. This was a gravel road that only took a mile or so off the commute, but it was a change of scenery and was quiet and little used. Along this road, about a half mile from our house, is a small cemetery that sits atop a rise in the land, surrounded by farmland. Although some of my ancestors settled here in the 1870s, I have no relatives in this small cemetery.

Early one morning a few years ago, I was headed up that road on the way to work when, as I approached the cemetery, an image appeared of people in the road. It was early and dark, and the truck headlights didn't reveal anyone, but the image was clear and stark. As I passed the cemetery, I also passed through something that is difficult to explain. I can't say that I believe in ghosts or such. I've heard others tell of experiences, but like UFO sightings, you have to see one to accept them as possible. The image that appeared to me that morning was of a small group of people, with a young woman in a flowing gown or robe. She appeared to be leading the group, which was mostly children, although there was an elderly man at the back. The group seemed to be crossing the road and returning to the cemetery, but from where I have no idea. They didn't seem to be moving, though, just frozen there in that single moment.

When I passed by the fence at the end of the cemetery, I hit something. Not the truck, just me. I had been willing to just chalk the image up to the early hour, but as the fence went by, I had something like a severe adrenaline rush, and I could taste something: it wasn't unpleasant, just very unfamiliar. I looked in the rearview mirror, but, of course, nothing was there, so I went on to work, and the day was otherwise uneventful. I thought about that image some, it seemed as though there was a look of concern on the young woman's face. Not alarm, just kind of worried, almost like she knew they had been seen. But maybe it had nothing to do with me being there at all, I don't know, but it gave me goose bumps.

On my way home that evening, I stopped at the cemetery. Most of the graves are for children, not uncommon for cemeteries of that time. The place seemed very peaceful: there is a small bench just inside the gate, a pile of brush as though someone had been caring for the cemetery and a great view of the surrounding countryside. I've been up and down that road a number of times, but that image only presented itself that one morning. I do remember though that the next growing season resulted in a large number of big hay bales in the field directly across the road, and I remember thinking about the people I saw and worrying that they can't get across now, but then, who can't get across, and why do they need to get across anyway?

A couple of years ago, as spring was in full bloom, I noticed that no had mowed that little cemetery. I called the neighbors to see if they knew who had been doing the mowing and was given the name of a gentleman. He told me the pastor at his church had been caring for the place but due to an illness he was unable to keep up with the mowing. I asked if it was all right if I did the mowing? He said sure, but don't you do enough on your place? I hesitantly told my friend of that early morning image, not knowing for sure what he would think about such tales. But instead of laughing, he offered me gas money and a spot in the cemetery if I wanted to be buried there, then asked if I'd be willing to help build a new fence. Seems as though a few years back, someone had left money for just that—a new fence.

So, I don't know if I adopted a cemetery or it adopted me, but I still mow the place, weed the flowers and get to eat a handful of wild strawberries that grow there each spring. It is a pretty place for this part of the country and is likely why this township is called Center View. It took me several weeks before I was ready to tell anyone, even my wife of thirty-eight years, about that image in the road, and even yet, every time I tell the story I get those goose bumps all over again.

16

A LADY'S HOUSE IS HER CASTLE

LILAC HILL

The house is tucked away above the road, behind a thick screen of shrubs that give both fragrance and name to the setting: Lilac Hill. One of the most gracious examples of antebellum architecture in the state, the red brick mansion is distinguished by fanlights, fireplaces, columns, carved details and pediments. The twin chimneys top both wings of the house, and hand-dug cellars still underpin the building. The plantation—for Lilac Hill was more than a farm—was built and maintained by slaves, and the home is among the most haunted in Missouri.

The builder of Lilac Hill, Alfred William Morrison, was a Kentucky native who, at age nineteen, migrated to Missouri. He thrived in the new state, working first as a surveyor and then climbing his way up through government as assessor, judge and sheriff. He was also sent by General Clark to expel the Mormons from Missouri and raised the money to do so from friends.

In 1851, his service earned him the position of state treasurer. Morrison married into the bedrock of Missouri, taking Minerva Jackson, age seventeen, as his wife on March 15, 1825, in a Baptist ceremony. She was the daughter of a veteran from the War of 1812 who served under Andrew Jackson at New Orleans and was a prominent Boonslick settler. The Morrisons were local leaders in politics and society until Minerva's death at age fifty, while her husband was serving in the state capital. According to her wishes, her body was returned to Lilac Hill for burial.

During the Civil War, Morrison declared himself a states' rights advocate and refused to take the "test" oath to the Union, which stated "each civil officer in this state…take and prescribe an oath…that he will not take up arms against the government of the United States nor the Provisional Government of this state, nor give aid or comfort to the enemies of either during the present Civil War." Besides refusing to recite the oath, Morrison resigned from his position as state treasurer and remained at Lilac Hill to sit out the war, although as a slave owner, he allowed his slaves to fight in his place. Morrison died at Lilac Hill in 1883.

Son James had taken over the day-to-day management of Lilac Hill during the war and continued farming after the hostilities ceased on the battlefield but apparently not at home. Lilac Hill sheltered a second Minerva—"Miss Minnie"—who was born sometime around 1846–48. She was niece of the first Minerva, and a more proper, prim spinster was not to be found in the Boonslick. Miss Minnie remained unmarried and shared the home with the rest of the Morrisons, including her cousin James. When James brought home his wife, Miss Minnie was horrified. The new Mrs. Morrison was the widow of a local doctor and, in Miss Minnie's eyes, had less than a sterling reputation. Minnie purportedly hated her and was never happy with her presence. Lilac Hill survived family squabbles but passed out of the family's hands in the 1950s. Though Morrisons and Jacksons no longer live in the home, it appears that the families still visit now and then.

Marsha Davis, her husband, Joe Jeff, and their family lived in Lilac Hill for more than ten years and experienced enough spooky encounters to convince even the most skeptical of visitors:

There were many occasions when I hoped for a quiet day or night, but I never felt threatened. One night, my husband and I woke up to hear a heart-rending wailing and crying. It seemed to be coming from the corner of the bedroom, but we thought one of the children was upset. Joe Jeff went to check, but he couldn't hear any crying upstairs. He went outside to make sure there wasn't someone in trouble, but there wasn't anyone there. You could only hear the crying in certain rooms of the house—the minute you stepped out of the room, you couldn't hear it at all. It was crying like someone's heart was broken. I wasn't scared, just sad. That happened at least a half dozen times while we lived there. My son heard her as well: I was coming home one night from the hospital after visiting my husband, and my son came running out, saying he had heard me crying and was worried about his dad. But I wasn't crying at all.

Other times at night, the family heard violent sounds of crashing and dragging from the attic, but they never found anything out of place, despite numerous attempts to track down the sounds.

The spirit seems to be fascinated by water, which has caused quite a few upsets in the house:

> *We had just moved here, and I went upstairs and found the sink running over and both faucets turned on. Another time, we were heading out the door for a vacation, and I decided to check upstairs and found the tub faucets running. Finally, one day the sink filled up and ran over, causing enough damage so I had to replace the ceiling downstairs. We had the plumber over several times, and each time he left saying he couldn't find anything wrong with the pipes. Once, he even joked and said we must have ghosts because nothing else explained it.*

Another time, hay haulers stopped to get some water from a pump on the property:

> *I was inside working when the men came to my door and told me that a lady in funny clothes had suddenly appeared and yelled at them for using the water and then was gone. I mentioned that it might have been Miss Minnie. They were shocked and left the property as soon as they could get the trucks moving.*

Each of the family members seemed to have his or her own experiences. One hot summer's night, Marsha's son was home with a family friend with the windows wide open for a breeze when suddenly they felt the wind blowing. Thinking it was going to rain, he got up to shut the windows but then realized that the wind was blowing inside the house, not outside. Another time, he was going upstairs to his room and felt someone walking up the stairs behind him. He was so terrified that he ran up to his room, slammed the door, climbed on the roof and slid down to the ground. He tapped at his parents' bedroom window and refused to go back to his room that night.

Joe Jeff was in bed one night when he heard footsteps and felt someone sit on the opposite side. Thinking it was Marsha, he rolled over to say something. But the bed was empty, and he heard someone say, "Don't worry, I'll only be here a little while." He was still in shock when he heard footsteps return to the door and then everything was quiet again. Even the family dog was shown some attention, Marsha recalled. "We'd put him outside and in a few minutes, he'd be back inside. The door was shut, and no one was there to let him in. But there he was."

The identity of the spirit—or spirits—remains a mystery. Lilac Hill has been visited by psychics who believe the house is haunted by several ghosts. Miss Minnie was particular about "her house and might be watching over it and its occupants. Mrs. Minerva Morrison could be back for a different reason," noted Marsha. "When we bought the house, we found her tombstone in the shed. Perhaps it had been replaced by a more modern stone at the Jackson Cemetery in Fayette, but I wonder if she is coming back looking for her marker."

And the wailing? Another family story might explain the eternal grief that has echoed through the house. In 1853, a widowed Milton Jackson (the first Minerva's brother) suffered a devastating loss. His two daughters, ages seven and nine, died within days of each other while living with his mother. The *Columbia Statesman* noted that poison was suspected, either by accident or by the actions of a family slave. Given the closeness of the family, could someone still be mourning the lost girls?

And an even darker possibility exists. Marsha used to think that the crying came from someone in the family. But she knows that the cellar used to have slave shackles still attached to the walls. "Whoever it is is just filled with grief. I've tried talking to her, but it didn't seem to help. I hope she gets some peace. I just hope so."

NEAT AND CLEAN

The reasons ghosts remain in a particular place are many: their tragic deaths, which they have not yet accepted; a connection with families and friends; or perhaps a curse that ties their spirits to the earth. In the Boonslick, ghosts seem to be firmly attracted to houses and places of earthly abode. Domestic ghosts prefer to remain where they are most comfortable—sometimes among the living—and if neither is aware of the other, then all is well. But it is when the two worlds overlap that connections are made and stories begin. And such was the case with one ghost in the small town of Duncans Bridge.

Just outside the city of Moberly, there stood an old house on Route 1 that had been owned by an elderly woman. The woman, who had weathered most of the nineteenth century, had been told by a doctor that she would soon die of heart trouble. Being of a practical mind, she decided to put everything she owned into the cellar and kept housekeeping upstairs as simple as possible. Her home was always neat as a pin, and she still swept out the house with a stiff corn broom and spun yarn on an old wool wheel. Her neighbors thought her eccentric, but she kept to her ways until her death not long after. The house remained empty for a time and soon claimed a reputation for being haunted.

Several years after the woman's death, Mr. and Mrs. Allen W. Fifer purchased the house, according to their granddaughter, despite its reputation. The Fifers were adamant in their dislike of superstition—they did not believe in ghosts—and so their first year in the new home was peaceful. Then, late one night, Allen Fifer awoke to a sound in the basement. It was loud enough to carry through the house and reminded him of a strong humming sound, rising and falling on the night air. He got out of bed, but at the step of his foot on the floorboards, the sound stopped. He rolled over in bed, only to hear the humming start up. Once again, he stood up and the sound stopped. Finally, he began to think about burglars but knew that the downstairs doors were locked and the basement was not easily accessed from outside. Finally, the sound seemed to fade away, and Mr. Fifer was drifting off to sleep when the rattling of china dishes began downstairs.

At this point, Mrs. Fifer woke, listened to the sounds and chose to bury her head beneath the covers. The two were terrified as they heard first the swishing and brushing sounds of a broom as it swept the floor and then the movement of items as someone dusted the furniture. The sounds went on for an hour, one after the other—dishes, broom, wheel and duster—until finally everything started up again at once, and it seemed as if the entire neighborhood was cleaning the cellar. Then, suddenly, the house was silent, and the Fifers waited for the comfort of morning's light.

Although they never heard the cleaning ghost again, the Fifers sold the house within a year and moved to a farm. The house is now gone, but local people continued to believe that the cleaning spirit still haunts the region, visiting barns and making certain all is neat and tidy.

Another Sort of House

While many ghosts haunt St. Louis, they are often younger ghosts, just starting their histories in the eternal. And oftentimes, the ghosts are upright citizens who suffered disaster—like the Lemp family, with a story worth telling if only because of their sad and eternal fall from grace and wealth. Or the Jefferson Barracks spirits, who still mark their night watch by challenging trespassers onto the post. But the Boonslick at St. Louis is home to other, less "honorable" ghosts as well, especially those in Mary Henry's house.

Mary Henry was a popular St. Louis madam, a former prostitute who owned a bordello on St. Charles Street (formerly Vine Street) in the mid-nineteenth century. Although she does not appear in the census records of the time—perhaps because she held so many secrets about city fathers—Madam Henry's "house" appears to have been quite popular with the local gentlemen. In a time when women had limited choices in life beyond marriage, the lucky few without family or husband might become governesses or schoolmarms, retaining society's respect. The desperate had little choice but the poorhouse or the streets, and once entered upon those lives, a woman could never regain her place in society.

One of the "inmates" of the Henry house knew this well. She had been raised a young woman of wealth and privilege, the daughter of a southern planter. A newspaper article of the era said that she had run off with the son of a minister, who abruptly abandoned her in St. Louis, where she joined Madam Henry's house and bade farewell to propriety.

This young woman may have been a soiled dove, but she appears to have met with success and was even popular among the other ladies of the Henry house. However long she worked for Henry is unknown, but she was still quite young when she succumbed to one of the many fevers rife in a river city. She must have found her life somewhat entertaining, because before she passed, she promised her sisters in pleasure that she would return from the afterlife for nightly visits. After her death, she was buried on the grounds of the mansion, but eventually word reached her family, who exhumed her body and brought her home to the family plantation. She may certainly rest in physical peace today along the Mississippi River, but at the turn of the century, it appears the young woman's spirit kept her promise.

Mary Henry's "palace of pleasure," as a local newspaper noted, lasted for a few more years and then was closed after her death. The building began a downward spiral from its former glory and finally, by the 1870s, the decrepit hulk came into the ownership of an elderly woman.

The house had been notorious enough to enter into the city's collective memory and was mentioned in an 1879 issue of the *National Police Gazette*, where "A St. Louis Ghost Story" followed the history of the Henry house and its ladies. The paper noted that since the 1860s, "at least a dozen mansions have become celebrated as 'haunted houses'" but "the only one which might be named without remorse" as having spiritual visitations was that once owned by Madame Mary Henry.

Of the elderly owner, a local journalist wrote, "This old woman reported that the house was frequented by spirits. She heard them every night going up and down the stairs, sometimes laughing, sometimes weeping, but generally in a mood of hilarity. One of these ghosts was that of a young girl who occupied a room on the second floor. The old woman heard the rustling of the spirit's dress and the pattering of footsteps every night as the clock sounded the hour of midnight, and sometimes she heard her sob and call despairingly upon some name that could not be distinguished."

The paper went on to note that steps had been undertaken to determine the truth of the tales. Even in the nineteenth century, ghost hunters attempted to prove or debunk the existence of spirits. One intrepid investigator rented a room in the old brothel and spent the night listening for the sounds of a haunting. He declared that the ghosts were only the result of rats, wind and horses chewing hay in the stable next door. Still, the stories persisted, and even the debunker returned for additional investigations and later agreed that the house was, in truth, haunted by the spirits of St. Charles Street. The house was torn down before the twentieth century arrived, but perhaps a modern exploration of the street is in order, for the young woman's ghost may still be enjoying her nightly celebrations.

17

DRINK TO ME ONLY WITH THINE CRIES

TWO HAUNTED TAVERNS

Taverns once dotted the Boonslick Trail, offering travelers a place to stop and rest on their way west over the prairies. The lodger might be traveling to Santa Fe or the Rocky Mountains for trapping and, later, to the California gold fields and new settlements of the Oregon Trail. Boonslick taverns were famous—and infamous—for their food and facilities. Strangers might find themselves sharing a bed with several other strangers for the night. The actor Noah Ludlow, who traveled the backwoods of the Mississippi Valley in the 1830s, recalled stopping at a tavern with fellow actors, where they shared a small room with two boisterous (and filthy) boatmen. The actors couldn't sleep, and they knew the only way to get some rest was to get rid of their roommates, so Ludlow and his friends waited until the drivers were asleep. Suddenly, the "ghost" of Hamlet's father appeared in costume, the other actors cried loudly for heaven's help and the boatmen awoke and fled down to the river, never to be seen again. The acting troupe slept well the rest of the night.

Today, the only remaining tavern on the Boonslick Trail is a log structure known as Van Horn's Tavern, which is awaiting restoration. It was a stopping place for poor and rich alike, including famous visitors such as Senator Thomas Hart Benton and Washington Irving, creator of Rip Van Winkle and Ichabod Crane. Van Horn's Tavern was a typical structure of its kind, with two smaller sections consisting of an upstairs and downstairs room and the downstairs sections connected by a dogtrot or breezeway. The rooms were about twenty feet square and included dining areas downstairs and beds upstairs. Food was plentiful, and drinks included rum, whiskey and cider, all guaranteed to make the evening fly by and the beds seem softer. Among the stories told around the fire were tales of ghosts, but this one may have been too close to home to allow the listeners a dreamless rest. Some say the setting was, in fact, Van Horn's Tavern.

Along the Boonslick Trail was a new tavern, built to serve the increased traffic of people who wanted to move to the rich lands of the Missouri interior. One traveler planned to stay overnight but woke the house by screaming that the tavern was haunted. His fellow travelers calmed him down, at least enough to hear his story. After he fell asleep, he was yanked back to consciousness when the bedclothes were pulled off his bed. He replaced them, only to have the blankets pulled down once more; the third time, the man held on to the blankets as an unseen being pulled with all its might and won the contest. Then the man heard sobbing and weeping in the corner of the room, saying that it sounded like a child in pain. Finally, a small, white figure floated up the wall, and the traveler fled the room in terror.

Very soon, the tale had traveled up and down the Boonslick Trail, and the landlord was unable to rent the room. He decided to try and spend the night there to disprove the story, but as soon as he fell asleep, the blankets were tossed away and a ghostly figure sobbed around the room. From that night on, the landlord locked the door and resigned himself to the loss of income.

One cold night, a circuit-riding minister stopped at the tavern. The landlord had no room at all for him, unless the minister wanted to stay in the haunted room. The minister, being a man of God, said he was not afraid of any spirits and would be glad to take the room over the discomfort of a blanket in the cold barn. The landlord opened the haunted room and showed the minister to bed. The reverend had barely settled down and extinguished the candle flame before the blankets flew across the room. The minister remembered his teaching: a ghost must answer if addressed in the name of the Lord. So, after calling out, "What do you want, in the name of God?" the minister listened in the dark. There came a child's voice from the wall, "I want a Christian burial. I was murdered and cannot rest." The minister was stunned but promised the ghost that he would try to find the body and hold services to ensure eternal rest. The spirit quieted immediately, and the minister slept the rest of the night in peace.

The next morning, the minister reported to the landlord what had happened in the night. Soon, men had torn a hole in the plaster wall of the haunted room and discovered the remains of a child. The minister dug a grave under the trees and consigned the child's body to eternity and peace, and the haunted room was quiet ever after. It seemed that the discovery finally brought forward a confession. A workman who had been plastering the walls while the tavern was being built was approached by the vagrant child for some food. The man said no and then, when begged again, struck blindly at the child and killed him. In a panic, he stuffed the child into the wall space and hid his crime by plastering over the body. There is no record that the workman paid for murder, but the child rested in peace after that, and the tavern was never troubled again by a ghost.

The Girl in the Corner

Jefferson City, Missouri, may be the state capital, but it had its less formal side as well. A river town once called Lohman's Landing, Jeff City was selected as the home of Missouri government as a compromise. It sat centrally in the state, equal distance from St. Louis and Kansas City (or Westport) and halfway between north and south. The state penitentiary was built in Jeff City in 1836, partly to serve as a way of maintaining the city's importance to the state, since there had been efforts to move the state capital to other cities in Missouri. The city suffered its first disaster when the state capitol burned in 1837, and many records of early Missouri history were lost. Like other river towns, Jeff City attracted many German emigrants, and visitors today can still see the older, gracious German neighborhoods with their Old World architecture.

Train service to the city was not in place until 1855, when the Pacific line was run from St. Louis to Jeff. The heavily loaded passenger train left St. Louis, stopped at Hermann and then plunged into the Gasconade River, with the loss of more than two dozen lives and scores of seriously injured. Incredibly, two days later, a rescue train sent to transport the wounded back to St. Louis also plunged into a river from a rain-weakened bridge. Consequently, Jeff City did not have train service until 1856.

During the Civil War, the city was held by the Union army and threatened at times by Southern troops. In 1863, builder Joseph Knaur erected a brick and stone building just west of the capitol on Main Street. The road led into Jeff City from Boonville and points east and from Kansas City on the west, and the building's owner took full advantage of the traffic. He opened a blacksmith and harness maker's shop to service the local travelers.

Paddy Malone's Pub in Jefferson City is in a building that began life just after the Civil War. The structure has held taverns, a blacksmith shop and rooms for more intimate business on the upper floors. *Courtesy Tess Montgomery.*

By the 1870s, Jefferson City had grown, and 700 West Main Street was converted into a saloon, called the West End Saloon. (Later, the building was nicknamed "First Chance–Last Chance Bar," since it was the first drinking establishment after Callaway, a dry county, and the last saloon in Cole, a wet county.) The saloon was a popular hangout, and local legend held that after Frank James was pardoned by the Missouri governor Thomas Crittenden, in autumn 1882, James stopped at the West End and had a celebratory drink. It was also known that a fellow could find female companionship of a certain kind—the "upstairs girls" were willing to entertain in the third-floor bordello for a price.

Over the years, the saloon became a less raucous, more respected neighborhood fixture, passed down from family to family, eventually changing in style, music and food to an Irish pub, which it remains today.

In addition to the liquid spirits, the current building, named Paddy Malone's, is home to some more metaphysical "hangovers." Owner Allen Tatman moved into the building with his family in 2003 and has experienced some strange events. Tatman and his wife, Marilee, were sleeping when they were disturbed by the sounds of something running back and forth in the living room. It wasn't the Tatmans' dogs, since they were in the bedroom. Allen got up to check on the ruckus, only to find no one in the room and nothing out of place—except for the squeaky toy, which was in the middle of the room and not where it had been when everyone settled in for the night.

Other spirits have made themselves more obvious to visitors. There have been reports of a man in nineteenth-century clothing sitting on a couch, only to disappear. A girl with long hair watches patrons from a corner of the dining room and then disappears, but there is no door by which to come and go and no one ever sees her cross the room. "I was in the bar one night," recalled Tatman,

> and one of the guys who works here was cleaning up for the night. I heard steps coming up the stairs, then saw the door latch raise and the door open and shut. But there was no one there. I called out, expecting to hear the man in the basement—but the worker came out from the back and said he hadn't been in the basement. I still don't know who it was, or what they wanted, but I know what I saw.

Today, the pub remains a popular community establishment, ghosts and all.

18

THE STEAMBOAT GHOST

Although Sam Clemens—whose pen name was Mark Twain—is always associated with Hannibal, Missouri, he also spent much time in St. Louis, where his sister and brother-in-law lived. Sam's niece, Annie Moffett, recalled her uncle's visits after his steamboat adventures, when he would burst into the house singing, his arms filled with gifts for the family and stories for the evening hours. Sam loved ghost stories and learned many of them from Uncle Daniel, a slave on the farm of Sam's uncle. Clemens believed in the paranormal. He had visions of death (including that of his brother, Henry, who died in a steamboat explosion), and as a child he experienced vivid dreams that resulted in sleepwalking. His mother, Jane, believed in spirits and ghosts and was said to consider herself a sensitive, one who could "detect" the presence of a person who had passed on.

Twain was inspired by two great river men: Horace Bixby, his teacher, and Isaiah Sellers, a pilot who wrote about the river for local newspapers. "Clemens was a good pilot," recalled Bixby during an interview late in his life,

> in spite of what the rest of the profession said about him. I soon saw that he was a smart fellow, and it was his brains that made other pilots jealous and led them to say that he did not know the river, that he was just an inspired loafer, or something of the sort. He was a good pilot, and he learned it from me.

Mark Twain never forgot his home state, and many of his stories are based on Missouri people and places. Here he has just received an honorary doctorate from the University of Missouri in 1902. *Courtesy State Historical Society of Missouri.*

Bixby and Sellers are both buried in Bellefontaine Cemetery, St. Louis, where people have reported hearing the faint sounds of a steamboat bell at night.

Since Twain's stories often mirrored his life experiences, there is no reason to expect that he made up this ghost but merely changed it a bit so as to preserve its anonymity in the afterlife. In fact, there were two Mississippi steamboats called the *Boreas*, and one sank in the 1840s with a loss of $60,000 in gold. The characters Ben and Joe turn up in other works by Twain, including *Tom Sawyer*. Finally, William Jones was first officer on the ship *Quaker City*, which Twain boarded for a trip to the Holy Land.

One snowy night, the steamboat *Boreas* was working its way upriver to St. Louis, fighting the wind and cold. It was pitch black, and pilot William Jones was steering through the night by instinct and knowledge alone. A riverboat pilot was expected to know every inch of the river, up and down, by sight, smell, sound, touch and sixth sense. Jones was doing just that when the captain entered the pilothouse and suggested he dock the boat and continue the voyage in the morning light. Jones was enraged. He was a pilot. He knew the river, and he yelled that not even the devil could stop him. Then, to the horror—and admiration—of the crew, Jones guided the ship through a tricky river bend called "The Graveyard." A new pilot took over for the rest of the night, and Jones left the pilothouse, never to be seen again. When he failed to turn up for breakfast, the ship was searched, and it was sadly assumed by all that Jones had slipped on the icy deck and fallen into the river, where his cries went unheeded in the storm.

The next year, Ben and Joe were assigned to the *Boreas* as pilots. All went well for the season until one stormy night. Joe was in the pilothouse and knew that getting the boat through The Graveyard was the mark of a master pilot. As he entered the bend, the storm intensified, and he could see nothing. Joe called for the engines to stop so he could get his bearings. After the ship quieted down, Joe was straining every sense to figure out where he was when a faint movement and the sound of dripping water caused him to turn around. Suddenly, the bell line was jerked hard, and below, the engineer answered the pilot's call and added more fuel, making the engines pulsate and thrum. His heart pounding in his chest, Joe felt the wheel spin under his hands as he was pushed aside. As he regained his balance and turned back to gain control of the ship, Joe froze in terror. There at the wheel stood William Jones—or what was left of him—with a grim look, a torn and bloody face, blank, staring eyes and water dripping from his hair and clothing.

In a minute, there was pounding at the pilothouse door and shouts from the crew, but Joe couldn't move a muscle. He was frozen to the floor. The specter said nothing but turned the wheel and rang for even more steam. Joe stood and watched as Jones steered the boat through the storm as easily as if it were a sunny June afternoon. Then, as if sensing the river's opening and safe water, the apparition stepped back, turned and walked through the door.

As Jones disappeared, Joe heard a clank and the sound of something falling to the floor. Finally, the door was shoved open by Ben. The crew had thought Joe would strike a log and sink everyone and everything, so the officers had raced to the pilothouse in an attempt to gain control of the ship. But when they reached the house, they found the pilot door locked from the inside. It opened only when the ship reached safe water, and those outside had seen no one exit the house. After the crew had returned to work, Joe collapsed onto the stool, swore Ben to secrecy and then chattered out the story like a madman. Ben thought his friend had gone insane under the pressure of piloting through the storm, but as he stepped to the door to call for help, he saw something on the floor, glinting in the lantern's light. It was a pocket watch, dented and damp, the crystal broken but still running. Ben handed it to Joe, who pried open the back and read the inscription: "To William Jones from his father." Neither man piloted the *Boreas* again, and both were known to fear the coming of a night storm for the rest of their lives.

The End. *Courtesy Tess Montgomery.*

BIBLIOGRAPHY

Christensen, Lawrence O., ed. *Dictionary of Missouri Biography*. Columbia: University of Missouri Press, 1999.

Dyer, Bob. *Boonville: An Illustrated History*. Boonville, OH: Pekitanoui Press, 1987.

Haden, Walter Darrell. *The Headless Cobbler of Smalletts Cave*. Nashville, TN: Kinfolk Press, 1967.

Irving, Washington. "The Legend of Sleepy Hollow." In *The Sketch Book of Geoffrey Crayon, Gent*. New York: Van Winkle, 1819.

Kingsbury, Lilburn. *The Hobby Horse Rider*. Available online at http://www.vaughan.org/bios/wtk/HobbyHorseRider/hhr-21.html (accessed May 1, 2011).

Levens, H., and N. Drake. *A History of Cooper County, Missouri*. St. Louis, MO: Perrin and Smith, 1876.

Paillou, Emile R. *Home Town Sketches*. Boston: Stratford Company, 1926.

Patterson, Nicholas, and John Mason Peck. "The Boon's Lick Country: Two Gospel Preachers Explore a New Settlement." *Bulletin of the Missouri Historical Society* 5 (1949): 443–71.

Randolph, Vance. *Ozark Superstitions*. New York: Columbia University Press, 1947.

Richards, John Thomas. *SORRAT: A History of the Neihardt Psychokinesis Experiments, 1961–1981*. Metuchen, NJ: Scarecrow Press, 1982.

Richardson, Judith. *Possessions: The History and Uses of Haunting in the Hudson Valley*. Cambridge, MA: Harvard University Press, 2003.

Rothwell, Dan A. *Along the Boone's Lick Trail.* Chesterfield, MO: Young at Heart Publishing, 1999.

Sampson, F.A. "Glimpses of Old Missouri by Explorers and Travelers." *Missouri Historical Review* 1, no. 4 (1907).

Skinner, Charles M. *American Myths and Legends.* Philadelphia: J. Lippincott, 1903.

———. *Myths and Legends of Our Own Land.* Philadelphia: J. Lippincott, 1896.

Van Ravenswaay, Charles, ed. *Missouri: A Guide to the Show-Me State.* New York: Duell, Sloan and Pierce, 1941.

Vilas, Jonas. "Old Franklin: A Frontier Town of the Twenties." *Mississippi Valley Historical Review* 9, no. 4 (1923): 269–82.

Wetmore, Alphonso. *Gazetteer of the State of Missouri.* St. Louis, MO: C. Keemle, 1837.

Selected Newspapers and Magazines

Boonville Weekly Advertiser

Columbia Missourian

Missouri Intelligencer and Boonslick Advertiser

Missouri Republican

Missouri Saturday News

Salmagundi, 1807–08 and 1819–20

St. Louis Reveille

ABOUT THE AUTHOR

M ary Collins Barile is a historian with a strong interest in the very lively nineteenth-century American West. She lives in the heart of the Boonslick, a stone's throw from the hauntings in this book. She believes in ghosts, especially if they have a great story to tell.

Visit us at
www.historypress.net

www.ingramcontent.com/pod-product-compliance
Lightning Source LLC
Chambersburg PA
CBHW060812100426
42813CB00004B/1042